W9-BOE-018

BUSY TODDLER'S GUIDE TO

ACTUAL PARENTING

FROM THEIR FIRST "NO"
TO THEIR FIRST DAY OF SCHOOL

(AND EVERYTHING IN BETWEEN)

BY SUSIE ALLISON

Creator of *Busy Toddler*

All rights reserved. No part of this book may be reproduced, transmitted, or stored in an information retrieval system in any form or by any means, graphic, electronic, or mechanical, including photocopying and recording, without prior written permission from the publisher.

Library of Congress Control Number: 2020936000

ISBN 9781943147854

Text copyright © 2020 by Susie Allison

Photographs copyright © 2020 by Susie Allison

Photo credits:
Page 288 and cover photographs by Chuck Allison
Page 14 photograph by Amy Martino of Amy Walton Photography
Page 15, 75, and 240 photographs by Dannie Melissa Wit of Abeille Photography

Published by The Innovation Press
1001 4th Avenue, Suite 3200
Seattle, WA 98154

www.theinnovationpress.com

Printed and bound by Worzalla
Production date July 2020

Cover lettering by Nicole LaRue

Cover photograph by Chuck Allison

Book layout by Tim Martyn

Many of the designations used by manufacturers and sellers to distinguish their products are claimed as trademarks. Where those designations appear in this book and The Innovation Press was aware of a trademark claim, the designations have been printed with initial capital letters.

All of the activities in this book are intended to be performed under adult supervision. Appropriate and reasonable caution is recommended when activities call for any objects that could be of risk, such as hot glue, sharp scissors, or small objects that could present a choking hazard. If you are unsure of the safety or age appropriateness of an activity, please contact your child's doctor for guidance. The recommendations in the activities in this book cannot replace common sense and sound judgment. Observe safety and caution at all times. The author and publisher disclaim liability for any damage, mishap, or injury that may occur from engaging in the activities described in this book.

To Fe and PK, the best actual parents a girl could ask for.

ACKNOWLEDGEMENTS

To my husband, Chuck, who walked side by side with me in our long quest to become parents—thank you for never wavering as we reached for this dream.

Thank you to my publisher, Asia, for giving me the best advice of my life: don't write a book (ironic, huh?). Or at least, "don't write a book until I start my own publishing company and come up with the blueprint for us." Thanks for guiding my life since 2016.

To Lauren, Beth, and Erica, the best "board of directors" a lady could ask for. You've shaped my motherhood (and this book) in more ways than I could ever count.

To my partner, Beth, from dayswithgrey.com, I am forever grateful for your support.

To my colleagues Kristina from toddlerapproved.com, Jen from mamapapabubba.com, Katie from happilyevermom.com, and Clarissa from playteachrepeat.com—thank you for activity inspiration and most of all, friendship.

To Sam, the miracle who made me a mom . . .

To Kate, the surprise of my lifetime . . .

To Matt, the caboose we needed to finish the set . . .

You kids are the best. Plain and simple.

Thank you to my community of support, both online and offline. Parenting is a journey best traveled with others and I'm so grateful to have had a village surrounding me.

TABLE OF CONTENTS

MY NAME IS SUSIE AND I DON'T REALLY LIKE PARENTING BOOKS

Don't worry, the irony isn't lost on me that this is, in fact, a parenting book and it does, in fact, have my name on it.

Parenting books are an interesting breed. There's either the "yup, kids are awful" books, the "you're an awful parent" books, or the "your child is a flower waiting for your calming wisdom to help it grow" books. Look, no offense to anyone who reads or wrote those books, but they don't really fit my life.

I've always wished there was a parenting book out there that went right down the middle and was filled with real information about day-to-day life with kids. You know, one that shared things like, "Yup, it's totally normal that your kid just licked that tree." I've decided to write that book and FYI, I have seen all three of my kids eat bark before and it's been fine.

I'm an actual mom. I have three actual kids and I actually really like them. I don't always love that they like to hang out with me when I'm going to the bathroom or that they ask for a second helping of dinner the moment I sit down (solid eyeroll), but they're still pretty awesome.

I also look at parenting life from a teacher's angle—it's given me a unique perspective and background for this job. I taught kindergarten and first grade for eight years, and I have applied my knowledge of education and child development to help my family flourish. Through my Busy Toddler website and Instagram account, I've also helped hundreds of thousands of others with quality parenting tips and appropriate learning techniques. I'm so honored to get to help you now too.

We live in a really interesting time to be parents and I don't think anyone who was a parent before us is super jealous about how things look for our generation. In the past, kids ran outside to play capture the flag. Today, kids are more likely to watch someone unbox a flag in a web video than to actually capture one.

Our parenting load is bogged down by social media perfectionism, academic pressures on our kids, and unrealistic expectations of what parenting "should" look like. The world is telling us that our kids are terrible, we're doing a bad job parenting, and we should feel all the guilt from this . . . but you know what? I don't buy it.

Maybe that's my parenting secret: I don't buy into the culture of guilt and excessive (and misguided) expectations placed onto us and our children.

I'm living with all the anxious conversations floating all around me, but I'm refusing to listen. I see all the same expectations on social media and feel all the same pressures, but I'm doing everything I can to block it out and focus on what matters most: my family.

I want to help you do that too.

My parenting book will feel a little different—gah, admitting this is a parenting book is the first step. I want to share with you the ins and outs of actual parenting life, thoughts on early childhood education, and nuggets of wisdom from my years of teaching and raising kids. I also promise to reassure you that your stage 47 clinger/toddler is normal, and most importantly, you are not alone in parenting. I want you to end this book with your head held high and some good ideas in your pocket to help things go even better.

It's hard out there right now, I know. But you don't need to feel so overwhelmed by it all especially when you've got someone else in your corner with you. We can take this one day at a time and walk the road together.

Susie

THE BEST ADVICE I EVER RECEIVED

I took the kids for ice cream one June.

They were 20 months old, 3.5 years old, and newly 5 years old, and it was a very impromptu ice-cream-for-lunch type of trip. The kind of trip that as you finish saying the words, "Let's get ice cream," you're already having cold sweats because you didn't really think this through and now you are fully committed. You can't un-ring the ice cream bell.

Three kids. One mom.

This is like one of those math story problems: if three kids walk into an ice cream shop with one mom at lunchtime and the wind is blowing from the west, which kid will drop their ice cream cone on the floor first? I was on pins and needles for the answer to that inevitable question.

Once I had paid and everyone was sitting and eating their ice cream, I assessed the situation and went for the old parenting pat on the back: "OK! So far so good."

I decided I needed a photo to commemorate the occasion because if it isn't posted online or texted to my husband, did it even happen? Plus, I was basically witnessing a miracle or at least a parenting urban legend of three kids nicely eating ice cream without incident. As I stood back to take the photo, it hit me like a wave. Wow.

The photo proof: three kids having ice cream. Modern day miracle.

Look how far we've come.

You see, a year earlier (when I had a 4-year-old, 2-year-old, and a very demanding 9-month-old), we never would have stopped for ice cream, not even with my husband in tow. In fact, I vividly remembered that a year earlier, we had tried to get ice cream cones and even had Grandma as backup to make it a three-to-three ratio of adults to kids. Even then it was a complete bust, a total meltdown, and it was the reason we hadn't gotten ice cream cones in a whole YEAR. Yeah, it was that bad of a trip.

And yet, here we were, a year later with a three-to-one ratio of kids to parents and we were fine. We were doing just fine.

Look how far we've come.

Before we had our first child, my husband's uncle mentioned the best and simplest parenting wisdom I've ever received:

> **"Just remember it's all a phase. Whatever is hard or bad, today might be the last day of that phase and tomorrow, they'll grow out of it."**

I have no idea why I took this picture before we left, but I'm so glad I did.

It is the most-true statement I have ever lived.

It's really easy as parents to get caught up in the moment—to see only the trees and miss the whole forest, and to forget that every day our kids are growing and changing and these moments we are in are just that: moments. They aren't *forevers*.

Times change. We all change. We all grow up. The kids keep getting older, but you know what else? We get more experienced in our parenting. My kids had changed so much in that year between ice cream cones, but just as importantly, I was a year wiser at parenting. It's easy to forget how new we are to this job too.

Thank goodness we all get the chance to grow up and get better.

Whatever phase you are in right now, whatever is weighing you down as a parent or challenging you to your core, today might be the last day of that. Tomorrow, the kids might outgrow it.

It won't always be this way or feel this way.

This isn't permanent. This isn't forever. It's just a phase. Keep walking, keep putting one foot in front of the other, and keep moving forward knowing that your child is growing up and you are growing wiser and those two things complement each other beautifully.

Tomorrow, you will be a more experienced parent with slightly older children and the phase might be over. That is a hope I'm always willing to hold on to.

THEY AREN'T FOREVERS

- The struggle of dropping a nap—every. single. time.
- All the teething . . .
- Transitioning a baby from a bassinet to a crib
- Having to ditch the baby swaddle
- My infant son's scream fests from 5 p.m. to 7 p.m.
- I Hate Having My Hair Washed era
- Toothbrush Standoff era
- Four-month stretch when my oldest only slept with the lights on
- "We can't go to a restaurant without a meltdown" phase
- "Don't know how to sleep long stretches yet" phase
- "Is there a reason why I can't start my day at 5 a.m. with you?" phase
- "Screaming baby car ride" phase
- Early days after potty training when they might go at any moment . . .

TAKEAWAY MESSAGE

Don't plan your life around the hard stuff or sit in agony over the things that aren't going well right now. Parenting is fluid and it's all just a phase. The ship will right itself eventually.

2

NO ONE ELSE IS WATCHING

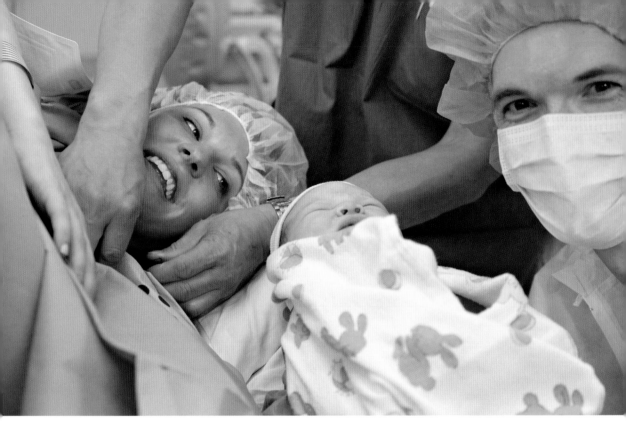

Our first family photo. What a moment.

I promise you: no one else is watching.

No one else heard your baby screaming in the store today.

No one else worried about your toddler's meltdown in the checkout line.

No one watched you struggle with the car seat.

No one else cared about the lunchtime standoff.

No one noticed you wore the same shirt yesterday.

No one saw that your hair wasn't washed.

No one cares that you didn't get a chance to vacuum.

No one knows you almost missed the day care evening cutoff.

No one cares that you didn't pack the healthiest snack today.

No one realizes you didn't brush her hair. Or your hair.

No one is offended if the outfits aren't matching.

No one is wondering what you fed your family for breakfast or if they've had enough vitamins today.

No one is thinking about your kids' bedtime routine or whether your kids even have a bedtime routine.

No one is questioning your parenting and judging every move you make outside your house.

Trust me. They aren't.

It may seem like the whole world has their eyes on you. You may feel like you're living under a microscope sometimes and a parenting professor is grading your life.

I promise, you are not and there is not.

Everyone has their own lives and their own problems. Cut yourself every bit of possible slack and remember, you aren't the only one carrying a load or trying your hardest to make it through the grocery store without tears.

You aren't doing this to gain approval from some stranger in aisle seven. This isn't about someone's supposed or assumed reaction to your parenting.

New mom Susie and new baby Sam.

We worry so much about what others are thinking, but they aren't the ones to focus on.

It's about you and your child.

Tonight, kiss your child on the forehead, hug them tight, and remember the only review you need to worry about at the end of the day is from the person with hearts on their eyes every morning when they see you again.

And I promise you: they're giving you a 5-star review.

TAKEAWAY MESSAGE

This is the lesson I wish I had known when I started out as a new parent: You are your harshest critic. What you notice and are hyperaware of probably isn't even a blip on the radar for someone else. No one else is watching.

3

PAJAMA FRIDAY AND HOW I GREW IN MOTHERHOOD

It's really easy to think we are sitting here in parenthood alone. That it's just us on an island of worry with a raft built out of complex emotions and Internet searches. I thought I was going to be pulled under by motherhood. This is the story of how I grew up in parenting with the help of my best friend and our pajamas.

I was so fortunate that when I became a mom, my best friend had also become a mom just 10 weeks earlier. How lucky is that?

The timing definitely was lucky, but it sure wasn't planned that way. I'd wanted a baby for years and after five rounds of in vitro fertilization, many cycles of infertility treatments, and all the shots, surgeries, and sadness, I ended up having a baby at the perfect time. It wasn't the timeline I would have picked, but I know now what the bigger plan was. And part of that bigger plan was that I was meant to have a baby and start motherhood with Jessica.

The overwhelming feelings of being a new parent is something I will never forget.

About a month after my oldest was born, I started going stir-crazy in my house. The feeling of being both incredibly busy while simultaneously having nothing to do was overwhelming. I didn't quite know what to do with a newborn, I didn't have my old job anymore, and I needed something for us to do. I also wasn't showering much or sleeping at all, and time seemed to stand still.

The days were dragging by and life was beginning to feel like a shampoo commercial: wash, rinse, repeat. It wasn't that I didn't love motherhood and feel so blessed to have FINALLY gotten my chance to "join the ranks," but every day was the same and I felt lost in it.

I was lonely. I was tired. I was overwhelmed with emotions.

It turns out Jessica was feeling the same way.

The best truth in parenting is one of the simplest: we are all feeling most of the same things. We are all facing the same questions, the same worries, the same phases, the same triumphs, the same struggles, and the same diaper rashes. But the key to everything in parenting life is talking about it and sharing how you feel.

By taking a chance and sharing how we were feeling as new parents, we discovered we both felt a little lost and a little lonely and needed a little help.

(Replace all the above "littles" with "a lot." That's a little more accurate.)

So, we made a plan. We took action to make our lives better.

Jessica and I agreed to have a standing Friday playdate—for something fun to do and to look forward to. Having just one thing on the calendar was enough to breathe life back into us. Our babies—both boys—were newborns so this playdate was 100% about the two of us. We needed each other. We needed to know we weren't alone.

We also decided to set up some ground rules so the playdate wouldn't become an overwhelming responsibility that only added more to our plate. This was about helping each other, not adding more to the drowning sensation we both already felt.

The simple rules:

- Every Friday
- Alternate hosting
- No cleaning beforehand
- No need to shower unless you want to
- Pajamas required
- No buying special food. We eat whatever is there.
- We co-parent (we help the other with everything)

Simple. Low-key. No stress. It was about support, not impressing each other with our hosting skills.

Pajama Fridays were born.

And that's how I saved my early motherhood while wearing pajamas.

We spent the next three years meeting every Friday. When I say this saved my parenting, I really mean it.

One of our first Pajama Fridays—so many years ago.

Because of Pajama Fridays, I had an outside source to bounce ideas off of and she knew my kid as well as I did. I didn't have to comb through the Internet or social media for advice. I had another set of eyeballs on the case.

When the boys were babies, we put their naps on opposite schedules—one down, one up, one down, one up. It was a riot of revolving naps and it worked like a charm. We'd sit and chat and watch TV and just be together.

In our pajamas.

Every Friday.

And it carried us for the whole week.

Sometimes, Pajama Friday would last all the way until one of the husbands got home. Mine would always laugh and say, "You two have fun now, but wait until there are more kids . . ." As the boys got older and the afternoon nap became crucial to our existence, we'd part ways after lunch and hope the boys would stay awake for the three-mile drive home.

One of the last Pajama Fridays (fully dressed and so much more confident).

Three years later, it was finally time to disband our long-standing Pajama Fridays. We'd each had three kids in less than four years. There were six kids and us. Pajama Friday looked a little different, but it still felt the same. And it still made our hearts sing.

During those years with all the kids, we grew up together as moms and gathered new superpowers and skills that we never could have imagined back when Pajama Friday started. Sure, the kids had grown up, but I think Jessica and I grew up the most during those years.

Back when we were first-time moms, tasks like getting dressed were challenging. Housework was out of the question. And we'd often work together to get dinner ready for the night. Many times we watched each other's baby so one of us could finally shower.

We had no idea how parents juggled multiple kids when we felt like we were drowning with one baby each and needed help just to stay afloat.

But then, almost magically through the years, tasks that seemed insurmountable in the early days of parenting were not only doable now, they were afterthoughts. We weren't just treading water anymore. We were full-on swimming.

With the kids in school, Pajama Fridays had to go by the wayside as life moved on. But now, in hindsight, I know those early years spent together parenting with Jessica gave me such a leg up and I'm desperate for other new parents to find that same help.

Text your friend today and see if they want to do a Pajama Friday. Meet a new friend through a local parenting group, a church gathering, or talk to your neighbor. Go out on a limb and find someone to get together with. Maybe it can't be every Friday, but even once a month will do. This cycle of loneliness and isolation can end with a single message.

The early years can be overwhelming. You will find your footing. You will also grow in your ability to do seemingly impossible tasks with great ease. It will happen. But I can't recommend enough how much more fun it is to walk this path with a friend sitting next to you in pajamas.

TAKEAWAY MESSAGES

1. You won't always be a new parent and you won't always feel like you are drowning. There will be a time when you won't have to strategically plan out when to shower. I wish I could tell you when you will magically cross over the line from then to now . . . just know that it will happen.

2. Put yourself out there, talk about what's hard, open up to a friend. Start walking the hard roads in parenting with someone next to you.

4

YOUR FRIENDS DON'T HAVE TO PARENT JUST LIKE YOU

I'm going to rip the Band-Aid off right now (no cutesy introduction here): **You and your friends are NOT going to parent the same way.**

There. I said it. It's the honest truth and it's FINE.

You and your friends might have the same outlook in life, you might have chosen the same college, and you might all choose to go to the same Justin Bieber concert together even though you're two decades too old to be there . . .

None of that matters when it comes to parenting.

You are not going to parent children the same way and there is nothing wrong with that.

PSA: You can be friends with people who parent differently from you.

That wasn't a joke. Here are my besties and me seeing Justin Bieber in our thirties.

It seems logical and intuitive, and yet, it's a really hard concept for parents to understand in this breast-versus-bottle, home-versus-day care, fast food-versus-organic world we live in. If someone doesn't have the same parenting views and beliefs as us, suddenly we start questioning who that person is.

Parenting is hard. It's complicated, it's messy, and everyone has different variables to work with. We have different kids. We have different lives. We have different philosophies.

We can value our friends and value their parenting even if they have the complete opposite of our own style. You can be happy your friends found a way that works for them. No one is asking you to parent your kids under their ideals—you can still do you.

I have friends with different philosophies on eating. *Awesome—I'm so glad all of our kids are fed.*

I have friends with different discipline policies. *You know how best to help your child recover from mistakes.*

I have friends with different feelings on what family time should look like. *I am so happy we all have families to be with.*

It's really easy in this stage of life to lose friends who don't parent exactly the same way you do—because we have this fantasy that we'll all do it the same way (or rather, they'll all do it my way). But you'll never find that. There's no perfect parenting soulmate out there for you . . .

There will also be plenty of friends whose parenting styles are compatible with yours. Instead of looking at the nitpicky points of parenting—the daily decisions—look for the overall values.

Do they care about their children? Do they care about yours? Do you feel safe when your kids are with them?

My friends and I might have different parenting lives, but when I'm with them, I know my kids are loved, valued, and happy, and theirs are too.

If we want to raise our children to have deep relationships with others (and I hope you do—parenting is way more fun with other families around), then we have to be willing to say, "I'm so glad things are working for you," and not worry so much about the differences.

As long as the overall values are there, the rest of parenting is a lot of fluff. Don't lose friends over fluff.

TAKEAWAY MESSAGE

Don't lose friends over things like baby sleep techniques or amber necklaces. Look at the big picture and remember these differences are actually a beautiful thing. When our friends don't parent exactly like us, it means they can share a different perspective that we maybe haven't considered yet. Value your friends and honor their right to parent how they see fit—and may they give you the same grace.

5

IT'S NEVER TOO LATE TO MAKE A CHANGE

It's not easy to read a parenting book.

I know—I've been there, I've lived it, I've done that. We want help and ideas so badly, but what we often find are chapters and chapters filled with (according to the author) the mistakes we've made and the irreparable damage we've done to our children (literally shuddering as I type that). We finish the book feeling a little defeated. *Sure, I've got some great new ideas now, but are my kids too old to make this change?*

Has the ship sailed? Have I missed the boat? Is it too late for my kids? Should I even bother trying something new?

Even when we want to make a change desperately, we wonder if it's too late.

Is there some magical window in parenting and raising children?

Are there hard and fast moments when we can no longer make a change no matter how much we want to?

Nope. There isn't.

If something is important to you . . .

If a shift has been laid on your heart . . .

If you feel like it's not going right and you want it to be better . . .

If you want parenthood and their childhood to look different . . .

Make the change.

Make it without any reservation. Make it without hesitation. Make the change, the shift, the new rule, the new policy happen immediately. You are the parent and this is your right. It's also your duty.

Do not for one moment worry that your children are too old to learn a new system or a new way of life. They are here to learn from you and be guided by you. You are older and wiser, and you know what needs to happen and what the long game is. Kids don't and they rely on us to make the best decisions for them even when those decisions are new or different or not what they would choose.

Make the change.

In everything you choose to do with parenting, remember you are the captain of this ship and you have every right to set it back on course if you feel like things have gone awry. Nothing is forever or permanent when it comes to parenting. It's fluid, always in motion, and can always be altered.

My family—I'll keep changing things up no matter how old they get.

Don't close this book thinking, "It's too late for my kids."

Don't close next week out thinking, "It's too late for my kids."

It is never too late when a great, involved parent is running the show. By opening this book, I know you are exactly that.

Change with kids is possible. They are resilient. They are pliable.

If it's important to you, that's all there is to it. No need to justify or second guess or wonder about timing. You are the parent. Make the change.

TAKEAWAY MESSAGE

Make the change. Could I be any clearer (wink)? You can do this. You are the parent. Stand tall. Talk with conviction, with confidence. Hold your head high as you make a shift for your family and know you are doing what you believe is best for them—and that, my friends, is exactly what being a parent is all about.

6

YOUR BABY
JUST BECAME
A TABY

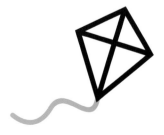

YOUR BABY JUST BECAME A TABY

(I promise that's not a typo. I didn't misspell a word and then publish it in a book. Although I wouldn't put it past me, so let's play a game called don't read too closely. My book editor is going to love me for this.)

> **Taby** (tay·bee) **noun**
> A made-up term to describe the time in early childhood development when a child has both baby-like and toddler-like qualities.

WAIT, WHAT IS A TABY?

On the morning of my oldest son's first birthday, someone said to me, "You don't have a baby anymore!!! Oh my gosh—he's a toddler now!"

I vividly remember thinking, "Well, that doesn't seem right . . ." but instead I responded with the standard glowing remark, "Oh, I know! They grow up so quickly!"

But I didn't know.

Sam's first birthday… definitely not a toddler yet…

The idea that he magically aged overnight didn't sit well with me. I knew in my heart that he wasn't a baby anymore, but I also knew he wasn't a toddler yet. How could this little boy who didn't walk and barely talked be classified as a toddler all of a sudden?

I didn't like it one bit, and not just in the "we parents want to keep our kids young forever" way.

I felt something was seriously wrong with the kid classification system.

It was as though the world was trying to shoo us out the baby door—like we'd stayed too long at the party. The problem was, I didn't feel like my son was ready to RSVP "Yes" to being a toddler.

Where did that leave us?

It left us in a weird limbo and, as all type A parents will understand, I needed a term for it. I needed to define it. I needed a name for where my son was in life.

There wasn't a name out there, so I did what I had to do. I came up with my own term and deemed my now one-year-old son a taby.

A taby has transitioned away from baby life but hasn't reached toddler status yet. They sit in a sort of developmental purgatory where they have some skills, but no real major skills.

It's a frustrating, hard, underrepresented, and confusing place to be—I know, because I've lived through "taby-hood" three times.

They're part toddler, part baby, and 100% taby. Nothing in the world is quite set up for them. Think about playing: there are baby toys and toddler toys. But what if neither is appropriate?

There are baby activities and toddler activities, but none of those fit either.

Taby Kate's claims that she didn't sample any of the edible paint were rejected.

It's basically like having a Goldilocks child with no third option that's *just right*.

When I had my first taby, I felt like we were stuck in some middle ground where I needed to pick one of two options: either wish he was older and had more skills or hope that he stays stuck as a baby.

Neither was going to work.

This idea that we needed to immediately graduate babyhood and move swiftly into toddlerhood didn't make a lick of sense to me. It felt like we were in a rush. (That's kind of the way childhood feels these days— everything is a rush.)

Taby Kate aka Baby Bucket Head

This middle ground—the Land of Tabies—is hard. It's frustrating for the parents . . . we know so much is just around the corner developmentally, but we feel a little stuck.

It's heartbreaking for the kids . . . they have a lot of the budding mind power of a toddler, but with none of the motor skills to make many (or any) of their plans a reality.

They are stuck in purgatory.

For me, the first step to helping this "problem" is to give it a name: Taby.

Having a name for this middle area feels like a move in the right direction to honoring these kids and their unique needs and skills.

For parents, setting this group apart from babies and toddlers is helpful because it lets us know we aren't making things up: this group is different.

It's like finally getting permission to treat these kids as the age group they are—not asking them to play up or down a bracket.

Just be tabies.

OK, BUT WHEN IS A KID A TABY?

I know you're trying to figure out when a child is a taby and what the hard and fast cutoff is. Is your child ahead or behind, were they a taby, are they a taby . . . is any of this normal?

(I kind of hit the nail on the head with that inner monologue, didn't I? It's like I've been a nervous parent before or something . . .)

Kids are tabies at various times—there's no hard and fast, black and white line that says "today you're a taby and tomorrow you're a toddler." It's a gut feeling. Kind of like choosing a good melon.

As the architect of this word, I feel I am at liberty to add some parameters that helped me decide when my kids were tabies (versus babies or toddlers). It's all my opinion, but here's what felt right to me:

Are they walking? When they walk has a lot to do with when they leave baby land behind.

Are they talking? How well they communicate has a lot to do with when they become a toddler.

We know that all kids achieve these milestones at different times and have different developmental paths because (say it with me) *all kids are different*, so here is a snapshot of when my kids (roughly) were tabies:

- My oldest was a taby from 13 to 23 months old.
- My daughter was a taby from 11 to 20 months old (she didn't have time for this).
- My youngest was a taby from 15 to 25 months old.

Taby Matt, dot stickers, and Dad's sock. Feels like the start of a joke.

USING THE TERM TABY MATTERS

Having a defined term for this phase actually matters a whole lot, and it's going to require me to briefly stand on a literary soapbox to explain it to you.

My book, my rules, my soapbox. Buckle up.

It's important to distinguish this group of children from toddlers, and here's why: assuming that a child has magically leveled up to the next age class on their first birthday puts us in a bit of a parenting pickle. I hate pickles, both real and metaphorical.

Look at this busy Taby Sam and his "Busy Board."

Let's imagine I have a 13-month-old child and I am told he is now a toddler. I know what a toddler looks like, sounds like, and acts like—but my child isn't that and now I'm slightly freaking out that I'm doing everything wrong. Suddenly, I'm heading down the path of "expecting too much," which of course is best friends with "now I'm worried my kid is behind" and "it's probably all my fault."

As a result, I now want to rush my child to meet some goals I mistakenly think they need to be reaching. Everyone is telling me my child is something they aren't and they're comparing my little one to children much older. My baby isn't acting like a toddler and now I'm worried I've done something wrong.

When we have expectations for our kids based on preconceived notions, it's easy to start worrying that we're failing or our children are failing. Please don't do that. I beg you. See your child for exactly who they are.

This is why having the word taby is really important.

And just like that my Taby Sam was Toddler Sam! Look at the difference in just six months...

Frankly, it takes the pressure off our 16-month-olds (and their parents). These kids don't need to be labeled as toddlers anymore. There's no expectation for them to behave in a way they aren't developmentally ready for.

They can just be tabies—little humans who have some growing skills, walk a bit like Frankenstein, and say a few half words. We can honor exactly who they are.

Expecting too much from tabies really puts a damper on enjoying a very magical time in childhood. These are the precious few months where they totter between two realms (baby and kid) and we get to enjoy every second of it.

We can use the term tabies and give a little space to this group. Let them be and develop on their own path without rushing to hop on the toddler train.

One day, you will wake up and realize your taby has finally turned into a toddler. This was always a bittersweet moment for me because at least with a taby there's a little bit of baby hanging on.

But once they move into being a full-blown toddler . . . you have to admit the baby days are over.

(I know. I'm crying about it too).

HERE'S THE 411 ON TABIES (A.K.A. WHAT YOU NEED TO KNOW)

They don't have long attention spans. Your taby will bounce from toy to toy, place to place, book to book like they are working the room at a political fundraiser. This is very, very normal. Taby brains move quickly to take in information and once they're satisfied with what they've learned, they move on. Nothing is wrong with your taby if they have a five-second attention span.

They don't need academics. This might seem like a no-brainer, but it comes up a lot. Tabies do not need rigorous learning activities because everything is a learning activity to a taby. The world is their learning oyster and we don't need to add flash cards to it.

They have horrible impulse control! It is what it is. They see it, they throw it. Life is a cause-and-effect classroom to them. We can help them learn to manage this and grow, but we don't need to worry they're destined to be a monster. Instead, we can acknowledge this growing impulse control as a skill. We can help them learn it rather than lament their lack of control.

They learn at different rates. Hey, this also goes for all kids, but we are in the taby section so we'll stay in this lane. Some tabies walk earlier, some later, and that won't make Kid A better at walking than Kid B when they head to kindergarten.

Expectations are different from milestones. Expectations are when we anticipate a child being able to do more than they can—this happens a lot with tabies. We expect them to have a longer attention span. We expect them to have better impulse control. Whereas a milestone is a developmental benchmark set by doctors and researchers to help catch potential concerns with kids and intervene if needed. If your taby is missing milestones, talk to your doctor.

They have tantrums too! Toddlers don't have the market cornered on tantrums— but with tabies, there's the added bonus of an even more limited vocabulary than toddlers. It's frustrating for everyone and that's OK to admit. Read more about tantrums in Chapter 11.

Guess what you should be doing with your taby every day? Letting them play, reading them stories, and having conversations with them. That's it! Don't stress about doing more or having some rigorous schedule to teach them. Play. Reading. Conversation. Make it your mantra. Make that what you hang your hat on each day.

7

TABY ACTIVITIES

I get it—keeping tabies busy is NOT EASY.

The attention spans are limited, the needs are high, and the independent play skills are just starting to form.

So what do you do when you need to entertain a taby?

Call me crazy but sometimes I really need to unload the dishwasher or make dinner or, I don't know, drink a cup of warm coffee that's only been microwaved twice.

That's where taby activities can really help.

These are quick and easy setups that can hold little attention spans so much longer—and by much longer, I mean 5- to 10-minute bursts (sometimes more). The mark of a true taby parent is knowing just how precious these 5- to 10-minute bursts of focus can be . . .

The goal with these activities is finding ways to both honor the taby's existing skills *AND* help them develop and learn new skills.

Remember, activities are like food: one day they like it, one day they don't. One day they hate it, one day they love it. Keep the activity out if it's safe for your taby and give them the freedom to choose the activity again later.

It's all about introducing activities at this stage and giving them chances to try new experiences.

> ## WARNING
> All activities need to be done under direct adult supervision. Use discretion for what is safe for your child and home. Reach out to your pediatrician if you have any questions about your child's safety with an activity.

TAPE RESCUE

SUPPLIES

- Small toys
- Tape
- Cookie sheet (or other flat surface)

HOW-TO

Grab a bunch of small toys and arrange them on a cookie sheet. Attach them to the sheet somewhat loosely using tape (I used painter's tape). Have your taby work to pull off the tape and the toys.

WHY IT'S GOOD

This activity helps with fine motor skills, cause and effect, and hand-eye coordination. It also gives your taby a goal (rescue the toys!) and a feeling of accomplishment when they meet that goal.

WHAT ELSE

Try playing this activity on an airplane. It's a great activity to set up on a tray table.

CARD SLOT DROP

SUPPLIES

- Recycled container (oats or sour cream containers work great)
- Knife (for prep and adult use ONLY)
- Deck of cards

HOW-TO

Start by cutting a slit into the lid. Make the slit large enough to fit playing cards into, but small enough so your taby has to push hard to get it to fit. Once they finish pushing all the cards through the slot, show them how to take the lid off, dump out the cards, and start over again.

WHY IT'S GOOD

Card Slot Drop helps with fine motor skills, cause and effect, and hand-eye coordination. It also requires some problem-solving skills because tabies need to orient the playing cards in the right direction to go through the slot. This promotes spatial awareness (their understanding of how objects are positioned).

WHAT ELSE

If you use a smaller container, like a sour cream sized one, Card Slot Drop is a great travel game.

STICKY WALL COLLAGE

SUPPLIES

- Contact paper
- Painter's tape
- Random recycled bits and craft trash

HOW-TO

Contact paper is fantastic (it's sold online, at dollar stores, and at "big box stores" usually as kitchen drawer liners). Peel off the protective backing and hang it sticky side out on the wall. Tape the edges to secure it into place.

Fill a box or tray with leftover crafting bits and pieces (such as cotton balls, paper, and pipe cleaners). Invite your taby to explore the sticky contact paper and make their own collage.

WHY IT'S GOOD

This is another activity for hand-eye coordination and fine motor skills. By hanging this on a wall, it promotes arm strength. This activity is also a process art activity—letting the child freely create.

WHAT ELSE

Leave it up for a few days—don't rush to put this activity away. Tabies bounce from place to place, so this might be one they bounce back to. It's a great way to promote independent play by having accessible options for them to turn to.

BATHTUB ART

SUPPLIES

- Washable paint
- Paint tray
- Paintbrushes
- Butcher paper
- Painter's tape

HOW-TO

Painting with tabies can be tough. It's hard to keep the mess contained. My advice is to paint in the bathtub. Cover the walls with butcher paper—make sure to cover the walls as high and wide as they can reach. You can also have your taby sit and paint the walls of the tub. At the end, turn on the tub to rinse them clean.

WHY IT'S GOOD

Anytime a child can work with their arms up and out is fantastic for muscle strengthening. It's not easy to work in that position! Having a child create art is also super important for their brain development and creativity.

WHAT ELSE

I prefer washable tempera paint for art activities. Make sure to test the paint on your tub or tile before blindly following the advice of some random lady with a book. Do your due diligence first.

TOY PUSH

SUPPLIES

- Empty wipes container
- Small (but not chokable small) toys or toy animals

HOW-TO

Show your taby how to push the toys into the slot to make them disappear. When they finish hiding all the toys, help them open the container to dump out the toys and start again.

WHY IT'S GOOD

This activity is rooted in cause and effect, and fine motor skill development.

WHAT ELSE

You can change this activity by switching the supplies your child is pushing into the container. With tabies, any little change means the activity is completely new and different to them. This is also a fantastic travel activity—it's an easy one to make up on the fly with random items you have lying around.

CORNMEAL POOL

SUPPLIES

- Plastic pool or giant storage bin
- Cornmeal (or uncooked rice)

HOW-TO

Tabies love a whole-body sensory experience. We can give them one with a giant sensory bin. I love cornmeal for how safe it is for tabies to taste, but it's also amazing to scoop and pour with. Your plastic kiddie pool from the summer is the perfect full-body bin. Fill it with a few cups of cornmeal for a unique play experience.

WHY IT'S GOOD

Cornmeal pools are a great way to learn about capacity (how much can I fit in this?), cause and effect (what happens when I dump this?), and tactile learning (how does this feel?).

WHAT ELSE

Do sensory bins give you the willies? No worries, I'll sell you on this idea. To learn more about sensory bins and kids, see Chapter 16.

SNACK HUNT

SUPPLIES

- Empty plastic eggs (Easter can definitely be year-round, trust me)
- Favorite taby snack

HOW-TO

Grab a bunch of plastic eggs. Bonus points if you can find an empty egg carton, but it's definitely not a requirement. Fill the eggs with a few of your toddler's favorite snacks or with some simple circle cereal. Put a lid on each egg and hand the eggs to your taby. You may have to show them how to crack the egg or give them a little tutorial on opening it.

WHY IT'S GOOD

This is just plain fun for tabies and stretches snack time out a bit, but it's also amazing for their fine motor skills and grip strength. It takes a lot of work to open a plastic egg. It's also a chance to learn more about cause and effect: when I open the egg, a snack falls out.

WHAT ELSE

Plastic eggs are really fun for tabies and don't need to be limited to springtime. In fact, online stores sell plastic eggs year-round. Tabies can hunt for them around the house, use them in the bathtub, fill them up in sensory bins, and eat snacks out of them (wink).

COLOR BATH

SUPPLIES

- Plastic water-safe objects and toys— ALL THE SAME COLOR
- Water
- Food coloring (optional)

HOW-TO

Wander your house with your taby collecting items that are all the same color AND bath time safe. Place all those color-themed objects in the bathtub and fill with water as per usual. Optional: add a few drops of food coloring in the same color for effect.

WHY IT'S GOOD

The best way to teach is through exposure and tabies LOVE learning colors. This is a great way to highlight a single color and give your taby some serious one-on-one time with it. It's also a fantastic way to pass the time during the day.

WHAT ELSE

Food coloring in bathwater doesn't stain. A few drops in that whole tub is massively diluted. But, as always, don't blindly follow the advice of a book lady. Make the decision that's best for you.

PEEL AND STICK

SUPPLIES

- Construction paper
- Painter's tape
- Dot stickers

HOW-TO

Tape one piece of construction paper to the wall. Any color will do. Hand your taby a sheet of dot stickers and let them decorate the paper. It's a surprisingly satisfying feeling for them to just peel and stick.

WHY IT'S GOOD

Peeling stickers is fantastic for taby fine motor skills. It takes a lot of work for them to peel off a sticker. Putting the paper on the wall gives the activity an added bonus—it works on arm strength too.

WHAT ELSE

To help tabies use dot sticker sheets, remove the white sticky part of the sheet (the part that surrounds the dots). This makes tabies roughly 600% more successful at peeling off the dots (that's not scientific, but it feels right).

RIPPING PAPER

SUPPLIES

- Recycled paper (gift wrap, construction paper, packaging)

HOW-TO

Put together a bin full of paper—all kinds of paper. Show your taby how to rip the paper into small and different sized pieces.

WHY IT'S GOOD

Ripping is a pre-cutting skill. It improves hand-eye coordination and grip strength. It is a surprisingly important activity for tabies to do.

WHAT ELSE

This activity might not look like much to an adult, but it's everything to a taby. It's satisfying, it's something they can be successful at, and it's a way to be independent. Tabies love ripping paper. Give the people what they want (and the people want to rip paper!).

8

WHY DOES MY KID LICK EVERYTHING?!

Apparently licking paint was like a rite of passage for my kids.

If there was a top 10 list of most often heard phrases in my house, "OMG, did they just lick that?" would for sure be on there. Probably top 5 even.

I have spent my life watching children, educating children, and now raising children and yet it still catches me off guard every time a child puts something to their mouth.

Where are my vomit emojis? I really need them right now in this book.

Here's the thing about licking: it is disgusting, it is frustrating, and it is TOTALLY NORMAL.

That's right: there's literally no way around this, people. It is completely normal (revolting, but normal) for kids to be licking and taste-testing things.

Can I get a collective ewwwwww?!

(Sigh.)

While it drives us all bananas, it's just a part of childhood.

And to answer your burning question: your child isn't abnormal for licking a window.

When a kid licks or puts something to their mouth, it means they're curious about what it is and they're trying to learn more about it using all available resources. They use their mouth as one of the ways to explore the world.

It's also because they lack impulse control. The thought pops in their head and they go for it. They don't have the self-control to stop their body from mouthing the shopping cart.

I'm so sorry I don't have a fix for you here. I'm failing Parenting Book 101 by not having a quick trick or cutesy simple idea to stop this. Not everything in parenting is readily "fixable."

I can at least offer some hope (which sometimes is all we need).

If you think back, you might remember that the baby version of your child used to put everything in their mouth. The whole remote. The entire rattle. The corner of the book.

Why does every kid lick baby wipes?

But now (I'm assuming here), now it's a lick from time to time or a quick sneak of this or that. They aren't trying to nor do they need to investigate everything they come in contact with—just the new stuff or the things they're really curious about.

As babies, they have no understanding of the things they get ahold of, so after careful examination in their hands, the next step is in their mouths. It's really pretty logical when you think about it. Gross, but logical.

Toddlers and preschoolers are beyond that and have a fair amount of background knowledge in place, so they don't need to explore the same way a baby does (yay!). But they still lack impulse control, which means they can't stop the behavior from happening once they think of doing it (boo!).

WHAT DO I DO WHEN THEY LICK SOMETHING?

Well, that kind of depends on the kid and their age. Usually, I say a very simple, "Yuck! Only food goes in our mouth." I don't yell or scream or scold. This is childhood curiosity and it is an impulsive reaction. Since our littles are learning to control their impulses, the best we can do is remind them not to lick non-food items and try to move on with our lives (no matter how disgusting it was).

Eventually one day, and I can't tell you when because it's different with all kids, they won't need their mouths to explore the world in a significant way (like the "put a pom-pom ball in their mouth" sort of way). They won't need to immediately taste everything that's new. They'll basically stop overnight and you'll find yourself suddenly going, "Hey! They haven't licked anything in a really long time!"

And just like that, the phase will be over. (Well, mostly over. I've seen some seven-year-olds lick some pretty questionable things in my day.)

If you have concerns that your child is overly oral and feel it might be part of a larger concern, please document the behavior and talk to your pediatrician.

A LIST OF THINGS MY KIDS HAVE LICKED

- Shopping carts
- Our street
- The seat on a Ferris wheel
- My kitchen chairs
- Most markers, some crayons
- The wall at a trampoline park
- A cat
- Several dogs
- One hamster
- The water in a touch pond
- Every slide in town
- A McDonald's door
- Their fingers at a petting zoo
- All of Disneyland
- Newborn brother in the hospital
- Old chocolate syrup on a Dairy Queen railing
- A toy saxophone at a garage sale
- The pole on the bus
- The railing on a ferry
- The seat belt buckle on an airplane
- Several restaurant tables
- Other people's children
- Me

9

WELCOME TO THE TODDLER SHOW

We were about 21 months into our relationship—my oldest and me—when he climbed into his newborn sister's infant seat to apparently take a load off from a busy day of following me around like a shadow.

He knew not to be in that seat. It had a low weight limit and he was 100% too big for it. We'd gone over this before. It wasn't new information for him.

"Hey bud, hop out of there. You're too big for it," I nonchalantly said.

And that's when it happened.

He looked me square in the eyes, adjusted his shoulders to make himself bigger, and said a very firm: **"No."**

(Insert stunned look on my face.) Um, excuse me, *but what just happened?*

This was not the cutesy "shake it off, wave it off, all done" sort of no that I'd previously heard from him.

This is the actual photo from the actual moment when Sam said no.

This was an opinionated, defiant, rebellious type of no—and for me, it signaled the beginning of his shift from taby to toddler. That moment when he asserted so much will and vocalized it so quickly was shocking and amazing . . . he grew up in an instant.

I felt a sudden shift between us, as if parenting was about to take a major turn. Where were we heading?

Too bad there was no cute sticker saying something like "first emphatic NO paired with look of complete disgust" to add to his baby book. I had to internalize this memory and keep it for myself. Oh and snap a quick photo, of course, to send to all the relatives.

It's one of those moments of parenthood I'll never forget.

This was a deeply rooted NO from a child who was previously so new to the world he didn't know he had an opinion to express.

But he did now. And everything was about to change.

I TRULY LOVE THE TODDLER YEARS

I'd heard every bone-chilling story about toddlers and terrible twos. Based on what everyone in my life had told me, I was sure we were about to enter a horrible, awful time in parenting. Anticipating this horrible phase was unnerving and unsettling and didn't help my psyche or parenting, because (spoiler alert): it all turned out to be untrue. It wasn't a horrible, awful time in parenting. It just wasn't.

Here's my goal: I can't go back and undo the thoughts and preconceived ideas I had about toddlers back then, but I can try to help some other parents (like you) see things a little different and enter these years with a much better perspective. A perspective I desperately wish I'd had years ago.

Matt and Me

More than anything, I want to help you understand that toddlerhood isn't this bad or scary time of life to dread or fear. As a collective parenting whole, we have to stop setting up new parents for that kind of self-fulfilling prophecy and expectation.

Let's start with this—if your child just said NO to you, or if they woke up transformed into a toddler, or if you suddenly realize the baby and taby days are officially behind you . . .

Sam and Me

Congratulations!!!!

No one really ever congratulates you on having a toddler.

They congratulate you for having a baby.

They congratulate you when that baby starts preschool.

They congratulate you when that preschooler begins elementary school.

But when you say you have a toddler, you typically get a look of sympathy, an "oh boy!," or a very sarcastic "Have fun!"

No one ever celebrates the toddlers.

Instead, we call it the terrible twos and tell parents that everything is about to go pear-shaped.

I'd like to change that.

Toddlers are amazing and I'll sell you on this. Don't worry. It's a long book. I have plenty of time.

Toddlers are fantastic tiny humans with thoughts, feelings, emotions, opinions, and approximately NONE of the skills to share those with you effectively. The way I see it, you're basically left with two options:

1. Believe that toddlers are terrible, go on the defensive, and run for the parenting hills.

OR

2. See the beauty in it, get really excited, and learn some tricks to help navigate our voyage across these seas.

That tiny person you've been dying to get to know is here.

The little bits of personality you've seen creeping up now and then . . . you're about to know that person. Toddlerhood is when things really start to shine. It is one of the coolest feelings in the world when you start to understand who your child is.

On the flip side, I also know and recognize that it is scary. This is a big unknown we're about to navigate.

We go to birthing classes and prep classes and we learn how to parent a baby, but what happens when that newborn grows up, has wild emotions, and throws a plate off the kitchen table? There's no swaddle technique to help with that.

It's easy to buy into the culture that toddlerhood is terrible and we just need to get through it, but friends, listen to me (I'm a three-time toddlerhood survivor):

We don't need to just survive this.

We can THRIVE in this and our kids can thrive too.

You officially have a toddler. Congratulations!

You just hit a green light on one of the most fun and fascinating times in childhood (and parenthood).

I am genuinely excited for you!

Kate and Me

DITCH THE TERRIBLE TWOS—IT'S A TERRIBLE SAYING ANYWAY

It only took me two rounds of the so-called terrible twos to realize something really important: these kids aren't terrible. Being two isn't terrible.

With my third-born, I had "seen the light" and knew exactly how age two would be. I promise I'll help you know this too, and it won't take having multiple children like it took me.

We were standing in the grocery store and my youngest was sobbing. His cookie from the bakery had broken in half and to him, the world was collapsing all around.

That cookie had meant a lot to him and he was now living in a toddler nightmare. Remember, cookies and broken things are very real and very devastating to toddlers. They might not be devastating to adults, but they are to kids.

He was full of tears and I was there to help him. Another customer walked by, saw a screaming toddler, and gave a knee-jerk response: "Oh man, the terrible twos! I remember that . . ."

I know she meant well.

I know she was just trying to be sympathetic.

I applaud her for reaching out to a young mom and offering a gesture rather than a sour look or eye roll of impatience . . . her heart was in the right place.

But the words weren't.

It wasn't that my son was being terrible. He wasn't terrible. Something terrible had happened to him and he was showing emotions about it.

There's nothing terrible about that.

Unfortunately, we live in a world where two-year-olds are deemed awful and that's so incredibly sad. It's given this group of little people a bad reputation and loudly says "they're terrible and that's all they can be."

I don't buy that.

I believe this is an amazing age and that we can rewrite the narrative on toddlers, which starts by rewriting the language we use to describe them.

The confines of the shopping cart were too much.

It's really easy to hunker down, tattoo "Terrible Twos" on our forearms, and put on some emotional armor against these children. After all, it's the only way we've been told to handle toddlers.

We are taught that the alpha-parent will win toddlerhood. Think of all the times you've heard:

"Just put your foot down."

"They need to be told no."

"Make them be quiet."

"Tell them to stop crying."

These kinds of phrases are so engrained into our parenting repertoire that we fall back on them quickly, easily, and without much thought.

Isn't that what we're supposed to do?

The term "terrible twos" gets so much traction because it's so darn catchy. The problem is, it's setting us up for failure—both the parents and the kids.

I'm not trying to insinuate you're failing as a parent or your child is failing. Don't misread that and pile on more parent-guilt than we already feel. No one needs that.

What I mean is, when we call it the terrible twos, we are accepting that two-year-olds are awful and terrible by choice. They aren't.

Let's think about it this way:

Would you choose to be a toddler?

Would you choose to have someone constantly telling you what to do? Would you like having almost no say in your day-to-day life? Would you want the decision to drink from a red cup or a blue cup to destroy your world?

No one wants to live like that.

Not you. Not me.

Not these "terrible" twos.

We need to shift our perspective or, even more important, take on their perspective. Look at the world through their lens. Everything feels a little different if you stand for a moment in your toddler's Velcro shoes.

We can do so much better by our kids if we shift to their perspective. We can acknowledge this is a hard time for them (and us!) without devaluing or demeaning who they are as people.

It took me until my third child to learn that two-year-olds aren't terrible, but it must be terribly hard to be them.

> **Wondering what more we can do than just stop calling this phase the terrible twos? Don't worry, my best tips for helping toddlers through tantrums and meltdowns and wild emotions is on its way (Chapter 11 to be exact).**

10

BEING TWO
IS FINE

It's all sorts of fine to hate an activity your mom lovingly made you.

Say it out loud. It'll make you smile.

Being two is fine.

It's fine.

Sometimes it doesn't feel so fine, but when you really peel back the onion layers on being two . . . it's fine.

It's fine if they want to wear the blue jacket, not the pink one.

It's fine if they want the ruby red slippers, not the sneakers.

It's fine if they only eat sandwiches cut into triangles and one day decide to switch to squares, but not tell you until you've already made your first slice. It's fine.

Friends, if you remember just one thing I say (or rather write) it's that being two is fine.

Two-year-olds are amazing. They are emotional. They are unpredictable. They have less life experience than some of the condiments in my refrigerator—and that perspective is easy to lose when they're on the floor in a screaming heap.

Back when my youngest was just about to turn two, things were getting all sorts of fine for us. His opinions needed to be heard . . . loudly . . . (I type with a smile on my face).

Having weathered the toddler storm twice before, I knew what was coming—what had worked in the past, what I'd do differently, and what I wanted toddlerhood to feel like this time around.

I wanted it to feel fine, and I wanted to acknowledge that these toddler moments are good and normal and fine. Being two is fine.

There's a frustration we ALL feel when raising a two-year-old. You are not alone in feeling this way and neither is your child. You are a good parent and all those frustrating moments are not a reflection of you or even them. Two-year-olds aren't bad kids.

In a world that tells us they are terrible, let's flip the script and instead say with confidence: "being two is fine!"

No matter what they throw at us (literally or figuratively), remember they're only TWO.

They've been alive for TWO YEARS (or use the number that's right for your child, because trust me, #being4isfine too).

Two years isn't even a substantial percentage of YOUR life, and yet think of all we ask of them and expect of them. It's really easy to forget just how young and new they are.

We need to do a better job of shrugging things off, having a laugh, seeing the beauty, taking a breath, and remembering that being two is not a direct attack on us or a targeted attempt to play mind games. They truly aren't doing this on purpose.

Stop and smile. Stop and acknowledge. Stop and think about what it must be like to start out in the world. We put a lot on the shoulders of these young kids and we expect a lot from them.

Being two is complicated, amazing, terrifying, exhilarating, hard, and fine.

Being two is fine.

It's all sorts of fine to wear big sister's ruby red slippers and carry an umbrella.

11

WHAT CAN WE DO ABOUT TANTRUMS?

Toddlers and tantrums are like emotional peas and carrots. They just go together.

We can all agree that two-year-olds got the "terrible" title because of tantrums alone. Anyone who is willing to throw their body on the floor, screaming, yelling, and kicking over a toy must be terrible, right?

Mmm, not exactly.

We can do so much better for our kids (of any age) if we first back the bus up and think about tantrums and meltdowns logically. We are adults, we have logic—we can look at this from a few different angles (as opposed to our toddlers who don't have the chance to be quite so logical).

I used to be so angry when my toddler threw tantrums because I flat-out didn't understand why he was acting that way. I felt manipulated by him. I felt overwhelmed. I felt like I was doing everything wrong, that he had caught on to my naivety, and that we were a doomed sinking ship.

Then one day, it finally dawned on me. I did a complete 180 and shifted my perspective on tantrums, which changed everything. I started looking at them in a whole new light.

THE LOGICAL LOOK AT TANTRUMS–WHY DO THEY HAPPEN?

Toddlers are in a tough spot. They have opinions. They have thoughts. They have hopes and dreams.

But they also have a very limited amount of resources or power to do anything with these feelings.

Frankly, that must feel really yucky.

The first move in shifting our perspectives on tantrums is to stop and imagine life as a toddler:

You live in a world where you speak a limited amount of the language and understand about half of what's spoken to you. You have feelings and ideas like everyone else around you, but no free will to act on them. Your hands don't work well, your legs and feet have limited mobility, and you have absolutely no idea how to tell the difference between a big problem and a little problem. Life is new and hard and full of challenges that no one else seems to be experiencing.

Think about what it must feel like to be a toddler or any young child for that matter. A toddler's life is a lot different from our life. They don't have the same free will, motor skills, and maturity that we have. They are in a much different position than we are and acknowledging those differences is huge.

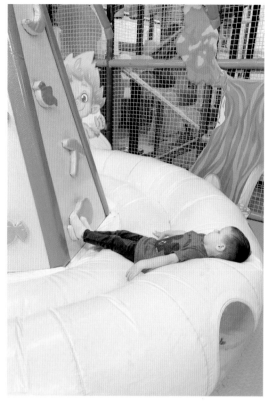

Forever my favorite photo of Matt taking a moment to think through life.

Like I said before, toddlers are in a tough spot. I can't imagine living the lives they do.

You see, tantrums aren't a reflection of you as a parent or your toddler as the worst child ever. Instead, they are a reflection of a brain, a body, a human that is just starting out in the world and doesn't have the same skills to navigate emotions the way we adults do.

It's OK that they have these big feelings.

It's OK when they need to show them.

What is not OK is when we adults expect toddlers to have the same emotional maturity, problem-solving skills, and impulse control that we do. They don't, but we forget that. A lot.

Our goal as parents is to teach them these things, which means understanding, accepting, and realizing they don't have these skills right out of the gate. They weren't born with them and guess what, neither were you.

You learned emotional maturity over time.

You learned impulse control from trial and error.

You learned problem-solving by watching and listening, and just plain growing up and getting older.

Can it still be frustrating when your toddler has a total meltdown? OF COURSE. But you can also start to shift your perspective because there are two big jobs we adults have during a tantrum and we need to focus on these:

1. Don't make it worse.

2. Look for the chances to teach.

(We'll get to exactly how to do those in just a second.)

LET'S IMAGINE HOW A TANTRUM FEELS TO A TODDLER

You're getting ready to leave home with your dad and he's saying things like, "We're running late. We need to hurry. We've got to go soon." You aren't sure what all that means, but he's moving fast.

He goes to put on your coat and you realize it's the one that itches.

You say no and try to explain that you don't want to wear that coat.

He keeps repeating something about being late, but again, you can't tell time so none of his words make sense to you. What does make sense is that coat itches and you don't want it on your body.

You keep saying no and hoping he'll understand. You don't have all the words to say, "That coat itches when it's on me and I'd like to wear a different, softer coat instead," so you just keep repeating no. You're getting more and more frustrated that he doesn't understand your needs and for some reason, he's starting to get really angry.

Everything is overwhelming. Your thoughts and feelings aren't being heard, you don't understand why your dad is upset, and you absolutely will not wear the itchy coat.

You lose control and all your feelings spill out as you crumple to the floor.

Living in a world where you have so few choices, so few words, but so many opinions must be so hard.

Toddler life is hard. Much harder than we give them credit for.

I know it's been a long time since you were a toddler, but you were once. We all were. This used to happen to us, but we've grown up. We do better now because we know better.

GUESS WHAT? YOUR TODDLER DOESN'T WANT TO THROW A TANTRUM

I'm here to let you in on a little secret about toddlers: they don't want to throw tantrums.

Throwing a tantrum means losing control and writhing in emotional pain. No one signs up for that willingly, not even a toddler.

It's easy to forget how much life experience and knowledge we have under our belts and how toddlers have exactly zero. Well, slightly more than zero, but you get the point.

Kate's silent protest at the park while she tried to bury herself.

When there's an adult problem, we have all sorts of tools to handle it:

- Measuring the size of the problem (is it worth it?)
- Considering the people we are talking to
- Examining the past and future of a relationship
- Using different tactics we've learned (like making "I" statements)
- Thinking through our argument logically

We adults do all those things when we are upset or having disagreements.

Toddlers. Can't. Do. That. Repeat after me: Toddlers can't do that.

Can you imagine a two-year-old making "I" statements at the park? "I feel like I should get to stay longer. I feel like I haven't played enough. I feel angry that we are needing to leave."

I'm laughing just writing those "I" statements, because frankly, it would never happen. We know it wouldn't and yet, when it doesn't happen (and the two-year-old starts screaming about leaving the park), we seem shocked at the turn of events.

Why do we constantly let the lack of emotional maturity of toddlers surprise us?

We have to remember that toddlers don't want to throw tantrums, but they don't have other ways to navigate their emotions until we help them learn how to do this.

> **How will toddlers learn these tools for handing disappointment, loss, and disagreement if we don't help them?**

If we go back to the example of the toddler and the coat, the root of that tantrum was not a manipulative child trying to pull one over on their dad. It was about communication, which basically accounts for all adult arguments too.

The toddler couldn't communicate their needs about the coat or ask questions about why their dad was rushing to leave. The child had no idea they were late (young children don't understand the concept of time), no idea how to explain the coat was itchy, and no idea how to solve the dilemma. Combine all that with the child not knowing about big problems versus little problems or how to handle disagreements, and you have a recipe for a tantrum.

Again, it's not because the child is bad. Or combative. Or manipulative. The tantrum happened because a very new-to-life human being was overwhelmed, confused, and didn't know what to do.

We can't erase tantrums or wipe them out altogether. Little brains will get overloaded and tantrums will happen. But here's what I can help you with:

- Navigating tantrums better, shifting your perspective, and giving you some tools for handling them.

- Shortening tantrums and limiting their severity by learning a few good strategies.

- Making tantrums a teachable moment for our kids and helping them learn skills by coaching them through these giant emotions.

Let's take tantrums by the horns. Let's face this head on. We can absolutely flip the script on them . . . we just have to know how to do that.

THE BEST TRICK FOR DEALING WITH TANTRUMS

Want to know the first step to easing toddler pain and helping them off the tantrum train? **Empathy**. Yup, it's not some big, complicated, or fancy trick. A little empathy goes a long way.

We already use empathy in the adult world, yet we often forget to apply this great diffusing strategy with toddlers.

Tell me this—when another adult is upset, do you stand over them, hovering, and tell them to get over it, move on, or say things like, "it's not that big a deal?"

It took me a long time to learn that empathy is the key.

Can you even imagine doing that? We wouldn't. But we do it all the time to children when they have (what feels to them like) big problems. We need to extend the same courtesy to our kids that we give to other adults in our lives.

The knee-jerk reaction of telling toddlers to dismiss their feelings, get up, or demand they stop crying has got to stop. I would feel miserable if my dearest loved ones treated me like that every time I had a problem. Being treated that way during your darkest hour cannot feel good. We have to do better.

We need to unlock the power of empathy. We already know so much about how to use it, but we have to be willing to use it with our children. They deserve empathy too.

Let your child know they are heard. Let them know you are listening. Let them know you care about how they feel.

Remember, when a tantrum is happening, you can put money on the fact that your toddler feels wronged or they feel something isn't going right. You can't change the way someone feels (and you don't need to agree with their feelings), but you can change how you react to it.

Letting a child vent or saying you understand they're upset isn't letting the child "win." It's saying loudly to the child: "I'm here. I value your feelings. I get it." What you are doing is letting your child be heard. You don't have to agree with them, but you can at least honor their right to have those feelings.

Lastly, there is a very big difference between giving in and buying a toddler the toy they're screaming about versus saying, "I know you wanted that toy. I'm sorry you're upset." I am always sorry my children are upset – they're hurt, they're in emotional pain. It doesn't mean I'm going to change my position, but I can empathize and say, "I hear that you're sad. I'm sorry you are sad."

To be honest, that's exactly what I'd say to my adult friend—I'd tell her I'm so sorry she's upset, even if I didn't agree with her. Why is it so difficult to apply the same empathy to a toddler?

MY GAME PLAN FOR HANDLING TANTRUMS

Tantrums come in all shapes and sizes and they happen for all different reasons, and contrary to popular belief, I don't think kids mean to have tantrums at the worst possible time. That's just Murphy's Law and sadly, I don't have a fix for that.

Instead, I have a basic blueprint—my tantrum game plan—for what to do when my toddler (or preschooler or elementary kiddo) goes down the slippery slope toward Tantrum Land. It's my step-by-step routine to navigate the tantrum, prevent it from spreading, and come out with some learning on the other side.

1. Take a deep breath and silently state your age and then the child's age.

I am 36. He is 2. I always do this. I bring the ages into perspective and remember that only one of us has the ability to make choices, handle emotions, and have self-control. The other is learning these skills (and learning them from me). This is go-time for modeling how to handle tough situations.

The ball is 100% in your parenting court at the start of a tantrum. If you begin to yell and scream, you've modeled for your child that yelling and screaming should be used to solve problems. This is the opposite of what we want our kids to do or learn.

The ultimate goal during a tantrum is to model appropriate reactions and interactions and not add any logs to the tantrum fire. I'm going to say that again: don't add logs to the fire.

Remind yourself whose turn it is to have a tantrum. My turn was back in 1985. It's not my turn anymore.

2. Remember that being a toddler is hard, and frustrating, but also fine.

There is nothing "wrong" with your child. This tantrum is not a reflection of them or a reflection of you. It does not mean you have a bad child or that you are a bad parent.

It means your very young child is having a hard time processing something. They've lost control. You have to help them get their control back. And you can't do that if you lose control too.

3. Remind yourself that NO ONE ELSE MATTERS during a tantrum but you and your child.

Don't worry for a second about what other parents are thinking.

Don't worry about the other shoppers.

Don't worry about the family members watching you handle a total meltdown at a birthday party (remember Murphy's Law—tantrums will happen at the worst time).

Instead, worry about your child and what they will take away from this interaction. Focus on them and what they need. The other shoppers are strangers who you will probably never see again. This is your child whose relationship with you is one of the most sacred on Earth. Of course, you know who matters here.

Put the blinders on and help your child. They're in emotional distress. Help them climb out.

4. Meet your child where they are.

When my child falls over in a tantrum, I stop what I'm doing. I recognize they have lost control and I get all the way down to their eye level so I'm not an imposing figure looming over them. Or I sit next to them as they lie on the floor and show them I am truly here with them. There's no height and space and size difference between us. Think of how you comfort a friend—you sit next to them while they vent. Do the same for your child.

This is the time to let the child know that I can be an anchor to bring them back down after they have lost control. I can ground their world from spinning. I can respect their feelings while continuing to uphold my parenting values.

5. Validate their feelings.

"You wanted that toy. You really loved it! You wanted it to come home with us!"

"You don't like those shoes. You really hate them."

Remember that validating their feelings doesn't mean you agree with them, it just lets them be heard. *My parent is listening to me. My parent understands my feelings.*

This also helps your child—who has a limited vocabulary—hear how we explain feelings without screaming. When you acknowledge their feelings, you're also modeling appropriate statements to them. It shows them we can say how we feel without yelling about it.

6. Hold off on the life lesson . . . for now

Talking about feelings, reactions, communication, and life lessons AFTER a tantrum is a great time to do so—but during one is a pretty bad time. It's like saying "I told you so," which no one ever needs to hear.

I want my child to hear me when I'm telling them about family rules or ways to talk kindly to others, but during a tantrum is just not that time.

We want our children to learn from a tantrum—good can come from this hard moment. But no one can listen when they're screaming. So wait on the lesson until you are ready to teach and they are ready to listen. Keep it simple and brief.

"If you don't like your shoes, you can say, 'I don't like my shoes.' You cannot throw your shoes."

7. Offer a chance to reconnect.

Hugs are powerful. Hugs can reconnect us when we feel so alone. Touch can be healing. Offering a hug is always a chance to let your child know that even in their darkest hour, you are there for them and your love is endless. I want my children to remember this when life gets really messy (in middle school and high school and beyond). The road to this connection begins today.

"Do you want a hug?"

I don't assume they do and I always ask for consent.

One of my own kids often does not want a hug when upset, but they always give a small smirk at the offer because the thought still counts. I always offer one later when the meltdown is fully over, and that hug is always accepted.

The setup: I was with my three kids at IKEA—a store I've personally had many adult tantrums in, so I understand deeply how it feels to lose control there.

The plan for that evening was to leave my older two kids at the children's play area and eventually swing back to drop off my toddler for a five-minute "trial run" to see if he was ready for that magical space.

I took this picture and texted my husband, "We'll be a little longer . . ."

Our plans changed because the shopping trip didn't go as expected (when does it ever at IKEA?), so I had to let my toddler know he would not be going to the play area. And more important, he would not get to play in the ball pit—which was his real goal.

Cue the melt down in 3 . . . 2 . . . 1 . . .

My toddler crumpled to the floor and started screaming.

"I want the ball pit!!!! I WANT THE BALL PIT." There aren't capital letters big enough to explain how loud and angry he was.

I stopped.

I turned to my six-year-old and four-year-old and said, "Wait here. He needs help."

I didn't say he was being bad. He wasn't. A total injustice had occurred and he was frustrated, disappointed, and angry. This also teaches my older kids about empathy—that we can care for others. We don't need to be mad at someone for having a hard time.

I sat down next to my son on the floor where he was writhing.

I did not say, "Get up, stop crying, we need to go." I did not grab him off the ground and force him into the shopping cart. I did not tell him, "It's not a big deal."

Instead, I validated how he was feeling. I let him know I understood why he was upset.

"You wanted to go to the ball pit in the play area and now we can't. I'm so sorry you are sad. That's just awful."

I wanted him to know that I get it. What happened to him was awful to him. Telling him to "move on, it's not that bad, stop crying" would only let him know how out of touch I am with his life and that his feelings don't matter.

They do matter.

In his life, it was a big disappointment. Since he's two and doesn't know how to reason through disappointment the way an adult can, it's my privilege and job as his mom to help guide him through the process and model it.

I sat for another moment while he took some time to process everything. Remember to give kids time to just think through it all.

Finally, I offered some connection: "Do you want a hug?"

Guess what? He did. And I whispered into his ear, "I am so sorry you didn't get to go in the ball pit. Let's make a plan to try that next time."

He squeezed tighter and said, "Yes!" and together we got back on our way. This entire scene took just two minutes. Imagine how much longer it would have taken if I had yelled or screamed or ordered commands, adding more logs to his fire. Imagine the hurt and sadness he would have felt.

I didn't worry about other shoppers because I didn't care what they thought. I cared about what my son thought and what he learned.

Later, we talked and I told him, "When you get mad and plans change, you cannot scream at me. We need to talk about how we feel. In this family, we don't scream at each other. You can say 'I'm upset' so I know how you feel."

I gave him that life lesson, but I waited until things were calm to make sure he heard me.

THE MYTH OF BEING A PUSHOVER

Empathy sometimes gets a bad reputation in early childhood, as if validating a sad or angry emotion somehow lets the child "win."

I'm pretty sure no one is winning during a meltdown. Not the parent trying to be a guiding light through the darkness nor the child wailing on the floor. That child is in pain. That child's brain has overloaded.

Instead, we need to show empathy. The same way friends show empathy to each other.

Empathy helps calm the fires—but anger, nasty comments, and dismissive language fuel the fire and send clear messages about our relationship with our child.

"My dad doesn't get me."

"My mom doesn't know what it's like to feel sad."

"My parents don't care what I'm thinking."

Showing empathy doesn't mean the toddler is winning. Showing empathy means having the ability to put yourself in someone else's shoes and make a connection with them, and that is ultimately what helps you both weather the storm.

You are not a pushover when you connect with your child.

You are not a pushover when you listen to their feelings.

You are not a pushover when you diffuse a situation calmly.

The name of the game is helping the child learn. We can't help them learn to navigate tantrums if we are having a tantrum too.

FIVE PHRASES TO AVOID DURING A TANTRUM

Stop crying.
What the child thinks: Crying is a bad thing. (It's not.)

It's not that bad.
What the child thinks: My feelings don't matter.

You are making me mad.
What the child thinks: How I feel makes my parents angry.

You should know better.
What the child thinks: I literally don't know better until you teach me.

Grow up.
What the child thinks: When I grow up, I won't be sad or feel bad like I do now.

FIVE PHRASES TO TRY DURING A TANTRUM

I see you . . .
For example, "I see you are upset about having your toast cut."

I hear you . . .
For example, "I hear you said you don't want to wear a coat."

What if . . .
For example, "What if I sit next to you and we work on this together?"

Let's make a plan . . .
For example, "Let's make a plan to try that next time we come here."

You feel . . .
For example, "You feel sad that we can't ride the train."

THINK VET

What's a good book without a catch phrase? Acronyms help when our brains get fuzzy. Nothing makes a brain fuzzy faster than a toddler in a meltdown. In those moments of hysteria, sometimes it's hard to remember all the tricks and tools we've read online or in an awesome parenting book (wink). We don't always have our wits about us, especially when it feels like the fate of an entire childhood lies in one moment (it doesn't, trust me—it just feels that way).

In those tough times, think VET: Validate, Empathize, Teach. It's simple. It's effective. It's a road map in tantrum management.

Validate: Value their feelings. Sure, you might not have realized that piece of toast meant so much to them, but apparently it did. Don't dismiss their feelings or tell them to stop having those feelings. Instead, validate them. Show your toddler you care about how they feel. Caring doesn't mean agreeing – that's important to remember.

Empathize: Show some empathy. When you tell a friend about the rough day you had, you don't want to hear, "Meh, it's not that bad. You'll be fine." We want empathy! And toddlers do too. "I'm so sorry your toast broke." A little empathy goes a long way.

Teach: Figure out what you want your toddler to learn from the tantrum and keep that in your pocket—for later when things are calm again. We can use tantrums as teachable moments to help stop future ones, but we have to remember to teach them later. For example, you might tell your child, "When your toast breaks, say 'I need help. My toast broke.' You don't need to scream. Tell me so I can help you." A simple lesson from each tantrum adds up to a whole lot of learning (you don't need to go overboard with college-level teaching—a little lesson goes a long way).

12

CODE WORDS ALL KIDS NEED TO KNOW

Kate, on her second birthday, about 10 hours before disaster. I wish I could go back and hug this girl!

It was my daughter's second birthday and she was a hot mess.

We were supposed to have a quiet dinner with my parents, she'd open some presents, and the next day would be her actual full-blown birthday party. This was just the beginning of a very big weekend for her.

Instead, what I had was a two-year-old throwing a full-blown tantrum and things spiraling out of control. I was mad, she had lost control, and the whole birthday night fell flat from an acute lack of happiness.

Looking back, I can see it so clearly—she was overwhelmed and stressed. She was confused. She was at her emotional limit. The moment was all too much.

Back then I couldn't see it. I'm so glad I can see it now and share it with you.

I wish I could go back and see her again that night. I wish I'd shown her so much empathy in that moment. I wish I'd asked if she wanted a hug, taken her somewhere quiet, and sat with her while she got out all her frustrations. But I didn't. I didn't know better.

About the time we ended the dinner, called it quits, and sent my parents home, I said to my husband, "I just wish she had a way of telling me she was overwhelmed without screaming and acting out for 45 minutes."

Obviously, that's every parent's wish during an emotional meltdown—that the child could calmly stop and let them know exactly what's happening before things get out of hand.

Wait. Why couldn't they?

I had a moment while sitting on my bed that night, wondering what tomorrow would bring. Suddenly I had a pie-in-the-sky thought: "I can teach her. She's smart. She's a good kid. She doesn't want to feel like this and I can teach her how to get the help she needs."

I made it my mission starting that day to introduce "code words" to my daughter. Yes, code words. Like a secret spy language designed around one very big mission: help my toddler give words to her feelings without having to go into tantrum mode.

Spoiler alert: it worked! Giving her code words made a significant difference in our lives.

WHY DO CODE WORDS WORK?

First off, we know that toddler tantrums often stem from communication problems. They are new little souls, fresh to this world, and it's hard for them to communicate their wants and needs or how they are feeling.

Even as they gain more and more language skills, this is still difficult for them. Heck, I know a lot of adults who struggle with talking about their feelings—this isn't a toddler-only thing.

Once our toddlers have some language skills, these key phrases and code words really come in handy. I taught my kids these phrases as a way to empower them and give a voice to their feelings *before* they fell off the emotional cliff into a tantrum. These phrases helped stop or avoid so many tantrums from happening.

> **Remember, if we aren't teaching these self-regulation skills, how do we expect our kids to learn them? Children don't learn self-control and emotional maturity without seeing it, hearing it, and even being directly taught it. Our job, as always, is to teach.**

Instead of hoping my kids will magically learn to control explosive tantrums without any guidance, I see this as a big part of my job: emotion guider. That's my new official title. I really like it. I'll add it to the list of all my other jobs at home, right between personal chef and chauffeur.

Without direct instruction in handling emotions, our kids struggle. One of the most important parts of parenting a young child is teaching these skills because they will have a major impact on their teen and adult years.

Around age two (give or take, you know your kid and their verbal and cognitive skills), I started teaching my daughter to use these code words and phrases as a way to signal that something was wrong and she needed help.

These phrases are often the life lessons I teach *after* a tantrum has ended. "Hey, remember how yucky it felt to be so sad at the grocery store? Here's what you could have said to let me know you were upset." And then we practice the code words over and over. We talk about them often. We bring them up regularly. I even use them in front of the kids as I name my own emotions and feelings. Model. Model. Model.

Without modeling and teaching, we can't expect them to miraculously grow in their understanding of emotions and self-regulation. Take the time to teach. It's worth it. We can give our children power to handle their emotional lives—this is important stuff on the road to maturity.

THE CODE WORDS

1. "I'M HAVING A HARD TIME."

These phrases all started with my daughter whose second birthday was just one of many exciting moments with her as a toddler. She got frustrated easily because she wanted to be able to run the world on her own, and she assumed she should already have all the adult motor skills shoved into her tiny toddler body. It caused a lot of sadness that she couldn't do things and she'd often spiral into a tantrum.

I taught her to say "I'm having a hard time" instead of throwing a toy or game that wasn't working for her. Having this simple set of words that conveyed her needs was empowering for her.

Every kid having a hard time at the end of every shopping trip.

She knew the phrase worked because it always resulted in an adult stopping, looking at her, and saying, "You're having a hard time. Can you tell me more about it?" Without falling on the ground in a heap of screams, this two-year-old talked about her feelings. She recognized she was having a hard time. She verbalized it. She was in tune with her body.

I was the human embodiment of the dancing lady emoji the first time she said it. Instead of throwing a tantrum, she calmly stated, with little tears in her eyes: "I'm having a hard time."

Wow, there was my moment. I had a clear opening to stop, sit, and talk to her about her feelings. We talked about what was happening around her and worked through the situation WITHOUT A TANTRUM. It was like we'd crossed a major bridge together.

Think of how this must feel for a child to suddenly have a simple phrase to communicate so much importance—it must feel like a whole new lease on life.

2. "I NEED A BREAK."

Being a toddler can feel really overwhelming, especially for an introverted one. This is a great code phrase for kids in large group situations—it was hugely helpful for my daughter at family gatherings, parties, and other large events.

It's been years since she learned this skill, and my daughter still often finds me at parties to let me know she needs a break from it all. The noise, the people, and even the energy can be a bit much for her and I get that (now). Remember how I mentioned her second birthday? She needed a break from all the festivities and attention but couldn't tell me.

Years later, she still knows how to advocate for herself, ask for what she needs, and get it. All because of a simple phrase we taught her to use when she needs a moment.

"I need a break."

At Matt's birthday party, a 2.5 year old Kate let me know she "needed a break."

It's a simple way for a child to communicate that they need a quiet moment alone—and isn't it amazing how we adults need those moments too? We often need a second alone at big events or during stressful situations and we know how to ask for it. Imagine if you had no way of communicating that need. That's what it's like for our kids and why it's important to teach them this.

We worked on this phrase with our daughter most often leading up to big events. "Remember, if you need quiet or feel like you're having a hard time with all the people around, touch my hand and say 'I need a break.' We will go take a break together." We practiced this over and over until she was able to use it on her own to get the break she needed WITHOUT having a tantrum or outburst.

This was so empowering for her to be able to communicate what her body needed.

3. "I'M UPSET."

It's such a simple two-word phrase and yet, it changes everything.

One morning when my youngest son was two years old, he became visibly becoming agitated at the breakfast table. I watched as his blood started to boil, but instead of reacting to his behavior, I calmly said, "I need you to tell me what's going on in your heart."

Months before, he never would have listened to that. He would have started a scream fest and I'd be left sitting next to a yelling child while he worked his way back down to Earth.

Instead, he stopped and gently said, "I'm upset." Great—this was information I could work with and we could go from there to figure out what upset him.

It turns out he was upset because he wanted peanut butter—not butter—and he'd asked for the wrong thing. I've been there and had moments like that too. I know exactly what it's like to ask for the wrong food or item and I could empathize with him in that moment.

We got it all cleared up with two words: I'm upset.

OTHER PHRASES TO TEACH INCLUDE:

1. "I'M STRUGGLING" to let you know they need attention and help working through a situation.

2. "I'M FRUSTRATED" to tell you they're really upset they can't do something or change the way something is happening.

3. "I NEED A HUG" to let you know that they're sad or scared and need immediate reassurance and a connection. This is huge for our kids who respond better to physical touch. They have a way to ask for what their body needs.

After the fair, Matt laid down in the kitchen and told me, "I'm struggling." I get it, buddy.

TODDLER TANTRUMS HAPPEN FOR A REASON

Tantrums don't happen because you have a bad kid who isn't growing up right. They happen because you have a small child with a developing brain that gets overloaded and overwhelmed by emotions. Children don't have the same tools in their life toolbox that we adults have, and it shows.

Our job is to teach them how to handle these frustrating moments. They will have a lot of them in life. Teaching self-regulation skills during early childhood is the best time to do it—when problems and feelings are much simpler than what they'll face in their teen years.

Adding in these code words and phrases is a simple change, but finally being heard is unbelievably empowering for a child who is used to being misunderstood.

Wouldn't it be life-changing for you to go from unheard and confused to heard and understood? Talk about an empowering turn of events for our kids. It must feel like a breath of fresh air . . . fresh, tantrum-free air.

QUICK TIP

Need help remembering the code words and phrases to teach your child? Write them on index cards and tape them to the mirror as a reminder. Review them each morning for yourself, practice using them in your life, and then begin teaching them to your child.

13

PRO TIP - SAYING YES IS A GOOD IDEA

Why is it easier to say no than yes?

Why is no always our knee-jerk reaction?

Seriously. Why is yes one of the most terrifying and least used words in parenting?

It's really easy to get caught in a rut saying no to our kids. They ask, we say no. They want, we say no. They do, we say no. It's quite a cycle.

As parents, we are the captains of the family ship and it's our duty and privilege to keep the ship on course. We navigate stormy seas, difficult situations, bad ideas, and obvious pitfalls like champions. We keep the ship floating and it means saying no . . . a lot.

But on the flip side, we are also raising FUTURE captains. We are raising future leaders, future adults, and future parents. We might be the forever captains to this current family ship, but we have to let our kids take the helm every now and then—for a ton of really good reasons.

I took this photo because Matt was covered in "yes." It didn't matter to me that he wanted to wear his mittens, pajamas, and fancy red shoes to dinner . . . but it mattered to him so I said yes.

I don't want my kids to always be dependent on me. I don't want my kids to always look to me for answers. They've got to learn how to navigate this world on their own and I am A-OK with that—which is why we have to say yes from time to time.

There are two reasons why hearing parents say yes is really important for kids:

- It improves their self-esteem and feelings of purpose.

- It helps build decision-making skills.

SAYING YES IMPROVES SELF-ESTEEM

You make all kinds of decisions for yourself each day. You decide when to wake up and when to go to bed. You decide what to wear, what to eat, where to go, when to leave, what to do, and how to do it. Wow—we make a lot of decisions each day and that's not even half of them.

How many decisions does your child get to make?

How many decisions are you making for them?

We need to let our children feel like they have some ownership in their lives—these are their lives after all.

We often feel the need to take charge and control every little detail of their life. Consider how that must feel for a child to constantly be told what to do.

I'm not saying you need to turn over total control to your child and say yes to chocolate for breakfast or let them decide when bedtime is—we can see the bigger picture of their health and well-being.

I'm saying look for itty-bitty little decisions that have no safety or health implications. Look for decisions that won't topple your whole family or parenting system. These are decisions that make no difference to you but make a *giant impact* in your child's life. Decisions like which shoes to wear or what kind of sandwich to eat. You don't need to go overboard with options, but letting your child pick between two choices (that you can live with and that are safe) does so much good for their mental health.

Ask your child for input on *their life*: "Do you want raspberry or blackberry jam?" "Will you wear the red coat or blue coat?" "Are you going to walk to the car or do you want me to carry you?"

These are easy decisions to hand over to your child, and the decisions give them some autonomy and a feeling of power and control. When they rely on us for everything and we are handing down order after order, it takes away some of their confidence and self-esteem. They need to have the chance to provide input and have that input be used. Give them a chance to make some of the choices in their day.

SAYING YES IMPROVES DECISION-MAKING SKILLS

Making decisions is a skill that has to be learned, developed, and exercised just like any other skill.

When my kids get to make a decision, that's one small step toward autonomy and one giant leap toward them not sleeping on my couch in middle age. Our children will not be with us forever. They will live most of their lives away from us. So what happens to the child who has never had to make a decision on their own?

> **It's OK to let our kids take their own reins.**
>
> **It's OK to take a step back and let them lead, even when they're toddlers.**
>
> **It's OK if they have to learn through a natural consequence.**

One of the scariest parts of parenting is seeing our children fail. It's hard for us. We want success for them almost more than they do. We often make decisions for them because we know better—we can see what's about to happen and we know failure is coming. We don't want them to fail, so we intervene and make decisions for them.

But we have to remember—especially in early childhood—how important natural consequences are and how necessary failure is to future success.

First, we want our children to practice making decisions so they can learn to make good choices. They can't do that unless we give them room to try.

Second, we want them to learn that failure is OK, that natural consequences happen, and that these moments of loss aren't the end of the world. These moments provide a chance to learn, do better, and try again. If a child never failed or experienced a natural consequence in early childhood, what happens when they're a teenager? How will they respond to failure in high school?

Our kids need us to let go and say yes to their ideas sometimes, even when we know what's coming. I'm not asking you to put your child in danger or let them make a truly risky decision. But if your toddler is refusing to wear a coat, it's OK for them to head outside, figure out they're cold, and come back to get the coat. Sure, it might cause a meltdown and a hard few minutes—but they just learned a lesson on their own. And as a bonus, they failed and learned it wasn't the end of the world.

Making decisions is a huge skill and our children can't learn it unless we explicitly teach it through opportunities. Opportunities we've said yes to.

Remember, toddlers live in a world where they're told what to do and where to be. Let them make some decisions every day and you will both reap the benefits of it.

My son was adamant that he wanted to wear his fancy shoes outside. I offered him some advice about puddles and wet socks, but he wasn't interested. He wanted to wear fancy shoes.

I said yes to wearing the shoes, knowing full well what was about to happen, and I did so in the name of learning a lesson.

Of course, the shoes got wet, the socks got soaked, and my son was angry. But that day he also learned that wearing the right shoes for the weather was important. It didn't matter how many times I told him. He needed to learn that information for himself, and me saying yes was a big part of that. As a result, he now makes much better decisions about the weather and his footwear—on his own.

We could have had an epic battle over appropriate footwear, with lots of emotions and me ultimately "winning" by forcing him into rainboots, but he would have learned nothing. Yes, I also had to deal with the consequences of this decision and the angry, crying toddler, but I'm an adult and I got over it. He was a toddler and needed this chance to learn. It was one of those inconvenient moments in parenting when I had to sacrifice some of my happiness and time for him to learn an important lesson, and that's enough for me. He got to make a decision, and he learned from that decision. That moment was huge. That yes was huge.

Here is a list of decisions I let my kids make that empower them, but I couldn't care less about (shhhh, don't tell them):

- Which jacket to wear

- Which shoes to wear

- Which pajamas to wear

- What goes on their toast

- What glass to have their drink in

- When to wash their body during the bath

- How their hair is styled each day

- Which book to read at bedtime

- Which snack to eat (from a parent-approved selection)

- What to play with

- Where to play (inside or outside)

The purpose of saying yes to our kids is not to undermine our authority or create a shift of power where the kids are in charge—far from it. Instead, kids gain independence, we show our kids we value their opinions, and we build them up as members of our family community.

We don't need to be scared of saying yes to the little things. Turn off the automatic no button and give out a few more yeses. It's a little change with a great big impact.

TAKEAWAY MESSAGE

As you go about your day, notice how many times you say no. See if you can find even three chances tomorrow when your child can make a decision or you can say yes to their request.

14

MY TODDLER DIDN'T LECTURE ME

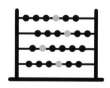

Do you ever have those moments where you wonder if your kids are already better humans than you? I had that happen to me one summer morning as I watched my toddler react to my mistake with far more grace than I had been showing him.

I was standing in the kitchen trying to put the cap back on a tube of flavored water tablets. As I was turning around to put the tube back in the pantry (while also still monkeying with the lid that wasn't going on right), I dropped all of it.

The whole tube went crashing to the floor, the tablets crunched everywhere, and the lid broke.

The moment it hit the floor, I let out a groan. "Oh maaaaaaan!"

I immediately heard the familiar patter of my toddler and his sing-song little voice coming into the kitchen.

"What happened, Mommy? You OK?!"

Look at him just helping me . . .   *His sweet little face—so genuine.*

I told him I was perfectly OK, but that I'd dropped the tablets on the ground, broken them, and made a mess.

"Ugh! I can't believe I did that."

My toddler didn't say anything. He just got on the ground and started helping clean up the mess. As his chubby little hands scooped up MY mess, I realized all the things he hadn't said to me.

At no point after I made an honest mistake did he say:

- What were you thinking?
- Why did you do that?!
- Be more careful!
- How could you!
- Look at the mess you made!
- I can't believe you did that!

Yuck. Those all sound eerily familiar.

Instead, my toddler asked if I was OK (he checked in with me first to see how I was doing and feeling), then he surveyed the mess and immediately started helping me fix the problem.

I was never scolded, reprimanded, embarrassed, or given any sort of life lesson about walking or carrying more carefully. I had made a mistake. I didn't mean for this to happen. He knew that.

He came to my aid.

He offered to help.

I wondered how many times I had forgotten to show him that much grace.

How many times had I scolded him when it was just an accident?

How many times did his new little hands just fail to work, and it wasn't his fault?

I know I can do better. Every day I'm getting better at seeing life from his perspective and remembering what this all must look and feel like from his angle.

At least he knows exactly how to handle a situation when someone makes a mistake.

TAKEAWAY MESSAGE

How many times has your toddler dropped or broken something truly by accident? Do they always need the lecture about being careful? We need to remember that accidents do happen. They happen to adults. They happen to kids. You would never scold your friend for spilling their water. Our level of compassion and understanding in these kinds of situations sends a very big message to our children.

15

TODDLER ACTIVITIES

I love a good toddler activity moment.

There's this myth floating around that toddlers need elaborate activities. That activities are only valuable and attention-grabbing if they are beautiful and gorgeous and totally camera-ready.

Like I said, that's a myth.

Kids don't need elaborate setups filled with fancy activity supplies and hours of their parents' time to put together. They don't need us working through nap time, painting, cutting, and gluing to create intricate activities for them to play with.

They need it be simple.

They need fun.

They need it to be engaging.

We can do all of that for cheap with things we have lying around our house, thrown together in a hot little second.

A note about ages: I hate putting ages on activities or dumping them into categories. Kids have different ability levels and different interests. I never want a parent to see an activity and be worried their child can't do it yet. Conversely, I wouldn't want someone to skip an activity because it's for younger kids. Activities are for all kids—whatever age the child can safely play with the activity and whenever the activity is right for them developmentally. I call these toddler activities—but that doesn't mean they aren't also perfect for preschoolers and kindergartners and 10-year-olds too.

WARNING

All activities need to be done under direct adult supervision. Use discretion for what is safe for your child and home. Reach out to your pediatrician if you have any questions about your child's safety with an activity.

TOY WASHING STATION

SUPPLIES

- Two storage bins
- Plastic toys
- Tear-free bubble bath (or body wash) and water
- Various cleaning supplies

HOW-TO

In the smaller bin, combine tear-free bubble bath and water to make the soap for washing. Set the smaller bin inside the larger one. Collect several plastic toys to wash. Give your toddler towels, sponges, and brushes to wash and clean the toys. Place them all on a large beach towel if there are worries about water on the floor.

WHY IT'S GOOD

This is a sensory activity where water is the base and kids are getting a change to learn a life skill (washing). It's also great for concentration, working to meet a goal, and independent play.

WHAT ELSE

There are LOTS of variations on this activity. Anything plastic can be washed! Wash the cars, trucks, baby dolls, animals, dinosaurs . . . even the kitchen plates.

SHAPE MATCH

SUPPLIES

- White butcher paper
- Painter's tape
- Sticky notes
- Black permanent marker

HOW-TO

Roll out the butcher paper to the desired size. On the paper, draw shapes (circle, square, triangle). Take the sticky notes and draw the identical number of shapes on those. Hide the sticky notes around the room and have your toddler race to find them. Once they find the shape, they bring it back and match it to a corresponding shape on the paper.

WHY IT'S GOOD

The obvious reason is that it helps shape recognition skills. But this activity also helps kids work on hand-eye coordination, visual discrimination skills (to see how the shapes are different), and setting a goal and seeing it through.

WHAT ELSE

Try this activity with letters, numbers, and number quantities (dot arrays) for toddlers and preschoolers. For bigger kids, try addition sentences, family member names, and sight words.

POM-POM SOUP

SUPPLIES

- Two storage bins
- Water
- Pom-pom balls

HOW-TO

Set a smaller storage bin inside a larger storage bin. Fill the smaller bin with water and add pom-pom balls (don't worry, they'll be fine). Adjacent to the bin, provide "cooking" utensils and more bins for play.

To dry the pom-pom balls, use a colander to strain the pom-poms from the water. Make sure to push out as much water as possible from the pom-poms. Pour them into a pillowcase and secure the end with a knot or rubber band. Throw the whole thing in the washing machine and dryer. Pro tip: it may take two runs in the dryer before all the pom-pom balls are completely dry.

WHY IT'S GOOD

This sensory activity is awesome for tactile learners and also gives a science lesson—pom-poms float AND fill with water. There's a lot of imaginary play involved to make this bin come alive.

WHAT ELSE

Want to be really adventurous? Set this up in the bathtub. I know . . . it's *that* amazing. *Please note that this activity includes choking hazards.*

DOT STICKER SORT

SUPPLIES

- Construction paper
- Dot stickers
- Painter's tape

HOW-TO

Hang up four sheets of construction paper: one sheet per dot sticker color. Remove the white sticky part of the sheet that surrounds the stickers to make things easier for your toddler. Have your toddler sort the stickers by color.

WHY IT'S GOOD

First, this activity is about sorting, which is an amazing skill for young children to develop. It's also a fine motor skills workout having to peel the stickers. The concentration and independent play levels are through the roof.

WHAT ELSE

Leave this activity up for at least an entire day with sticker sheets waiting. This is a great activity for toddlers to bounce back and forth to.

SCOOP AND TRANSFER

SUPPLIES

- Uncooked rice
- One large bowl
- Small bowls or cups
- Measuring spoons
- Storage bin to catch spills

HOW-TO

Pour the rice into a large bowl and place it in the storage bin. Next to the bowl, place small empty cups or bowls. Have your child scoop and transfer the rice from the large bowl to the smaller ones.

WHY IT'S GOOD

This is called a "life skills activity," meaning it helps a child learn a skill they will use throughout their life. Scooping and transferring materials is an important skill to develop.

WHAT ELSE

Vary the setup for this activity by using beans instead of rice, or cupcake tins and ice cube trays instead of bowls (see page 124 for tips on keeping this activity tidy).

ANIMAL LINEUP

SUPPLIES

- Painter's tape
- Animal toys

HOW-TO

On the floor, use painter's tape to make rows and designs for your child—think zigzag, vertical, horizontal, or tracks. Have your child line up their toys on the tape as a sort of toy parade.

WHY IT'S GOOD

It's meticulous, intricate work that takes lots of concentration and time. While kids are building their lineups, they are transported into a land of make-believe and play. This activity breeds independent play.

WHAT ELSE

Try this activity with cars, toys, puzzle pieces, or anything. Leave it out for your child as an invitation to play, and let them take the lead.

ICE PAINT

SUPPLIES

- Ice cubes
- Paint and paintbrushes (I like washable tempera paint)
- Storage bin

HOW-TO

Fill a storage bin with ice cubes. Let your child paint the ice cubes. The paint freezes slightly as it hits the ice for a very cool effect.

WHY IT'S GOOD

This is both a sensory activity and an open-ended process art activity. Kids get a chance to paint and interact with science at the same time.

WHAT ELSE

Ask your child what they notice as they play. What's happening to the paint? How is the ice changing? Why?

PUZZLE BIN SORTING

SUPPLIES

- Chunky puzzles
- Uncooked rice
- Two storage bins

HOW-TO

Fill a small storage bin with rice. Dump in the pieces from three chunky puzzles and mix them up well. Set the smaller bin inside a larger storage bin to catch spills. Have your child search to find the right pieces for each puzzle.

WHY IT'S GOOD

Puzzles are amazing for children and help them improve their spatial awareness. This activity also helps children with hand-eye coordination, visual discrimination, and sorting.

WHAT ELSE

Puzzle sorting is perfect for kids who have outgrown chunky puzzles, kids who love chunky puzzles with all their heart, or for those who might not be as into them. Revitalizing a toy with a sensory bin is a great way to breathe new life into it.

TUBE RUN

SUPPLIES

- Paper tubes (from toilet paper, paper towels, and gift wrap)
- Painter's tape
- Pom-pom balls
- Bowls

HOW-TO

Collect paper tubes and tape them to the wall to create a system for your toddler. Experiment with angles and different designs. Have them roll pom-pom balls through the tubes into bowls.

WHY IT'S GOOD

This is a great chance for toddlers to learn about systems (how parts work together to form a network). It's also a lesson in cause and effect, gravity, and motion.

WHAT ELSE

Keep your tubes on the wall for a few days and continue to add to it. Changing the design makes it fresh and new again for toddlers. *Please note that this activity includes choking hazards.*

GRAB & DROP

SUPPLIES

- Pom-pom balls
- Empty bottle
- Tongs
- Tray

HOW-TO

Place some pom-pom balls, a set of tongs, and an empty bottle with a large opening into a tray. Have your toddler use the tongs to grab each pom-pom ball and drop it into the container.

WHY IT'S GOOD

This activity is amazing for fine motor skills and it increases grip strength. It's also great for hand-eye coordination and concentration.

WHAT ELSE

Remaking this activity for each holiday has become a tradition. We glue construction paper to make the bottle look like a turkey, snowman, or a bunny for various holidays. The kids take turns "feeding" the bottle pom-pom balls. *Please note that this activity includes choking hazards.*

SINK OR FLOAT

SUPPLIES

- Large storage bin
- Miscellaneous objects (all water-safe)
- Bowl
- Water
- Food coloring (blue because my toddler demanded it; this is optional)

HOW-TO

Gather up a bunch of water-safe objects. Give your child a bowl of water set inside a large bin to catch spills. Tell them, "Today we are going to discover if something sinks or floats." Show them what it means to sink or float. Have them make a guess before testing each object. After they test it, have them place the item on the appropriate sink or float side of the bin.

WHY IT'S GOOD

This activity is an introduction to the scientific method for kids. Show them the supplies, have them make predictions, and share their conclusion. It's simple but effective.

WHAT ELSE

This is a great activity to keep in your back pocket—it's awesome in the pool, the bathtub, and outside. A new set of objects makes the activity brand new again.

COLOR MATCH

SUPPLIES

- Dot stickers
- Paper tube
- Markers

HOW-TO

Draw marker dots in the same colors as the stickers spaced out all over the outside of the paper tube. Draw as many dots as there are stickers. Hand your toddler the sticker sheet (with the white background sticker portion removed) and let them work to match the sticker dots to the marker dots.

WHY IT'S GOOD

This is a sorting, matching, fine motor skill, as well as an independent play activity for toddlers. It also helps with spatial awareness as they'll need to twist and turn the tube to find all the marker dots.

WHAT ELSE

It's easy to increase the challenge level on this activity for kids who are ready for a little more. For instance, you can write letters on the tube and the dots for an ABC matching activity. You can also try numbers, math problems, or spelling words.

16

MY FAVORITE PARENTING TRICK IS THE SENSORY BIN

Sensory bins are a staple in my house, but not just because I love watching kids scoop and pour rice. Sensory bins hold a much higher purpose in my parenting and also in my kids' personal development. They're more than just something for kids to play with.

Take every toy from my house, but leave the sensory bins. Sensory bins and blocks and maybe a few stuffed toys. One truck. OK, you know what? Don't take my kids' toys, that was a bad example.

Just know that in the hierarchy of toys in our home, sensory bins are number one . . . by a long shot.

What makes sensory bins so great? Um, everything. I promise I'm about to sell you on this. Buckle up.

This is a sensory bin:

This is a sensory bin and it's totally simple, nothing fancy.

Basic definition of a sensory bin: A tub or bin with a set of materials placed inside that children can interact with for tactile, hands-on learning. Sensory bins are often filled with rice, beans, cornmeal, or water, along with various other supplies and utensils for open-ended play.

I know that sensory bins can look intimidating—it's a bin of mess and you set it in front of a child who likes to make a mess. What could go wrong?! I get it. I know how this all sounds. I know that from the outside looking in, sensory bins are kind of hard to believe.

See? Even more nothing fancy!

THE THING IS, SENSORY BINS ARE INCREDIBLE FOR LEARNING

When it comes to kids, sensory bins invite an unbelievable amount of learning—like an over-the-moon, out-of-this-world, truly inspiring amount of learning. Yes, it looks like a child scooping and digging in rice, but it's so much more. This is play-based learning at its finest. Look beyond the simplicity of a sensory bin to all the learning a child is achieving.

While a child is playing with a sensory bin, here is some of the learning they're doing:

- **Life skills:** Sensory bins teach kids skills they'll use throughout their life, like scooping, pouring, measuring, and transferring materials.

- **Motor skills:** When kids use a sensory bin, they're using a lot of fine motor skills and doing some intricate work with their hands.

- **Math:** Sensory bins are full of math—capacity, volume, weight—in a real-world setting.

- **Science:** Depending on the material used in the bin, the science varies. In a water bin, it might be learning about liquids, displacement, and vortexes. With a rice bin, they're learning how particles move and learning about the properties of solids.

- **Dramatic play/imaginary play:** Kids create, discuss, imagine, and invent using sensory bins.

In a nutshell, sensory bins are powerful for kids and an easy way to invite a whole lot of learning into the house.

But even with all that, there are still TWO more reasons why I have sensory bins available to my kids every single day.

1. They hold a child's attention. For like hours. Days. Weeks. Nothing can capture the focus of a child quite like a sensory bin.

For starters, sensory bins are ageless. You can use them with kids from 12 months old to 12 years old and every age in between. Yes, even a taby who is still taste-testing the world can try a sensory bin—don't worry, we'll get to that. Adults love sensory bins too. . . mini Zen gardens are just fancy adult sensory bins sitting on a desk.

I can't entirely capture in writing all the magic that sensory bins are, so I ask you to please try them. First, I make you read a book I wrote, then I make you try sensory bins. I know. I'm running out of "asks."

If you have a toddler who is glued to your side and you can't figure out what to do to get them playing independently, the answer is a sensory bin.

If you have siblings who aren't playing well together, try a sensory bin.

If you need a way to calm a child down . . . guess what? SENSORY BINS.

We call this a "whole body" sensory bin experience.

Sensory bins have a way of getting children engaged like nothing else and it is beyond us adults. We cannot see the fun in a bin of rice. We do not see potential in beans. Cornmeal does very little for us unless it's in bread form next to some chili. *But it means something to kids.*

The point is you might not understand why I'm asking you to do a sensory bin with your child, but they will.

You need to blindly trust the Internet lady who wrote a book until you see sensory bin magic in person. Take the leap of faith. There is a reason you see them all over social media. There is a reason every preschool has a sensory table. There is a reason I've dedicated an entire section of this book to my love of sensory bins.

They are so important for kids.

2. Sensory bins help kids learn self-control.

I didn't put a sensory bin chapter in a book just because I love them that much. I mean, I do and I did . . . but there is a higher purpose.

Impulse control and self-control are important skills in early childhood and sensory bins can actually help kids learn these too. When the child is playing with a sensory bin and gets the urge to throw rice, eventually (with guidance and teaching) they'll calm the impulse and go back to playing without throwing it. They'll exhibit self-control. Self-control they learned by playing in a sensory bin.

Sensory bins give parents a great low-key opportunity to work with kids on self-control and rule following. Look, I'm not trying to make an army of children who will blindly follow me around and do everything I say because I'm a dictator parent.

Not exactly.

Kids need to have self-control, follow rules, and learn to play within those rules just like adults do. As an adult, I would love to go speeding down the road whenever I feel like it, but there are rules about speeding and consequences for not following them.

The same goes for the world of kids. There are rules and there are consequences.

Oftentimes, kids need to follow rules in very heated, high stakes, emotionally charged moments and you find yourself just needing them to listen, like when you are in a busy parking lot or walking down a dangerous road.

To me, sensory bins are a way to practice following rules and teach the child to have self-control (to live within the boundaries), but in a setting that isn't highly charged or life-threatening.

By enforcing sensory bin rules (I'll get to those next!), we're giving our children the chance to practice following rules and to exhibit self-control. When else do kids get to do that in such a fun setting? It's really easy to forget these are learned skills too.

Sensory bin play also gives parents a great chance to practice being firm and consistent. When big moments happen, when big boundaries come up, I want my kids to remember and know that Mom means what she says, she says it clearly, and she always enforces it.

There's a larger lesson here for everyone, it's not just about rice bins and sensory fun. We can teach our children about rules, we can teach ourselves how to enforce rules, and we can really learn together. All from sensory bins.

They told me "we need funnels and cornmeal." Sounds good to me!

THE SECRET TO ENFORCING SENSORY BIN RULES

Sensory bins look terrifying from the outside, but we know all the good they do for kids. This isn't fluff. We've established how valuable they are.

There's the play-based learning, the attention-grabbing awesomeness, and the chance to help kids learn self-control and impulse control. Sensory bins rock, but also: **How do we avoid messes?!** How do we keep sensory bins from being a social media fail photo?

Great questions, easy answer: just don't let it be a disaster (wink).

What a terrible answer. I'll give you more. I promise.

> **Sensory bins are all about firm, clear, and consistent boundaries. That's the secret to making them work and it's the same parenting secret for all of raising kids: Firm, clear, and consistent boundaries.**

If we boil down the best tips and tricks in parenting—concentrating only the most important bits—having firm, clear, and consistent boundaries with our children would rise to the top of any chart.

Every aspect of parenting depends on how well we apply firm, clear, and consistent boundaries. I'll keep repeating it so you commit it to memory. Firm, clear, and consistent boundaries.

Think of all the times in a day we lay out rules with our children:

- Bathtime—Keep the water in the tub.
- Dinnertime—Food stays on our plate. We do not throw food.
- Busy street—We stay on the sidewalk. Hold my hand.

We state these rules, we enforce them, we have kids live within these rules. And how do we explain them? Firmly and clearly, and we enforce them consistently. It always goes back to that.

So much of how we parent our children comes down to how well we communicate with them. Without firmness, our children have no idea if we are serious. Without clarity, information gets mixed up. And without consistency, our children don't know when something is a rule and when it is not.

Above all else in your parenting life, audit your messages to your children and repeat those three words to yourself: Firm. Clear. Consistent.

Applying firm, clear, and consistent boundaries to sensory bins not only makes the activities doable and manageable, but it lays the foundation for future rule-following.

Make it your creed, etch it in stone: I will use firm, clear, and consistent boundaries in parenting. You can start with sensory bins.

SETTING UP SENSORY BINS FOR SUCCESS

Intimidated by your toddler having four pounds of rice on your carpet?! What could go wrong?

A lot . . . I know!

When we set up a sensory bin, we have to be proactive for both ourselves and our children. This is a chance for them to learn amazing skills through play AND to practice impulse/self-control. We promote this learning by setting up a sensory bin with firm, clear, and consistent boundaries.

There's no fancy or extensive list for kids and sensory bins. It comes down to three components:

1. The setup

2. The rules

3. Enforcing those rules

Sensory bin rule #1 is no eating . . . Taby Kate took this very seriously (don't worry, I'll explain what to do).

Sensory bins really are magical (I know I've said that a lot) and your child can be successful with them.

Sensory Bin Setup:

- Have a generous-sized bin for your kids (check out my supply list on page 280). Small bins make for bigger messes because there's no room to play.

- Set a blanket under the bin. This provides a clear boundary for the activity and a fast way to clean up at the end. It makes life really easy.

- Be present to supervise. Until your child is old enough and has a certain proficiency with bins, it's never a good idea to walk away and hope for the best. Trust me. Stay close.

- Have an exit strategy. If this is an activity that will require handwashing or a bath afterward, have the exit mapped out ahead of time. Be your own flight attendant. Know where the exits are.

The Rules:

There are just three rules for sensory bins (and they're really basic and simple). Before my kids begin a sensory bin (even before they could talk) I always repeat the rules of the bin:

1. No eating

2. No dumping

3. No throwing

"No eating. No dumping. No throwing." By keeping the list short and light, I can repeat it quickly and easily. My kids (once able to communicate) can repeat it back to me. There's no ambiguity on the rules. They know them, they state them, they follow them.

Enforcing the Rules:

Arguably the most crucial steps in the process (as it is with all things parenting): enforcing the rules and having follow-through. Our goal is always to be firm, clear, and consistent. This takes away the guesswork for kids: they know the expectations.

But what happens when they aren't following those expectations? We've given the firm rules. We've said it to them clearly and restated consistently, but now what?

Now we have to enforce it.

We sit close to our kids as they are learning sensory bin etiquette to help them be successful. We can remind them of the rules, we can help guide their hands, we can be there to intervene.

Depending on age and knowledge of sensory bins, I give one to two warnings. "We do not eat from the bin." "We do not throw the rice." If those impulse control issues start to creep up and they do it again, I calmly pick up the bin and remove it. I set the bin in my laundry room and we try again later.

Here's Kate proving just how relaxing a sensory bin can be.

The stance. The concentration. The steady pour. This is a sensory bin win.

This might be five minutes from now, five hours from now, five days from now (however, I strongly recommend sooner rather than later because kids need an immediate chance to correct their behavior. A second chance goes a long way.)

It's not fun having a crying toddler or screaming preschooler who is upset because their sensory bin was removed. Consequences are important—they're part of the boundaries of life. These are the hard parts of parenting. We can see the bigger picture of how important impulse/self-control and rule-following skills are to learn.

When ready, state the rules again. For this second chance, I typically skip warnings (this is a parenting decision for you to make based on your child). Sometimes, it's just not a good day for the child's self-control and that's that. We don't need to lecture or be angry. They're learning and this is part of the learning process. They can help with clean up and have a chance to play another day.

The goal is always firm, clear, and consistent boundaries. Be firm. Be clear. Be consistent with how you present sensory bins and how you react when an issue arises. Our kids need to learn to follow rules, and they need help with impulse control. Growing self-control skills is huge. We can help our kids learn these skills through a sensory bin.

My two-year-old was sitting with a rice bin. We started by saying the sensory bin rules together: "No throwing rice, no dumping rice, no eating rice." The boundary lines had now been set with clarity.

She loved her rice bins something fierce and spent about five minutes playing without incident—five minutes is an eternity of peace at that age. Suddenly she grabbed a handful of rice and must have thought she was at a wedding in 1987. She began tossing it everywhere.

I immediately put my hands on her hands and said firmly, "No throwing rice. When you throw it again, I will take the bin away. No throwing rice." I enforced the rules quickly, and also firmly, clearly, and consistently.

She lasted about three more minutes before another handful went sky high.

I picked up the bin. I said to her tiny precious angel face, which was turning red with ensuing tears, "The rule is no throwing. We will try again later." Firm, clear, and consistent boundaries.

That's all I said. She knew EXACTLY what she had done and then saw the natural consequence of this action. I moved the bin to the laundry room and calmly shut the door. She cried. She wailed. She went into a total meltdown because that's what happens when we mess up. We get embarrassed, emotions go through the roof, and it's hard. I sat with her. I held her.

Since this is a learning process and we are working with playing within the rules, I wanted to let her have an immediate chance to try again with the sensory bin. After she had calmed down and things had leveled out, I knew it was time to give her that chance.

"I am ready to let you try the bin again. Are you also ready? Let's remember the rules. No eating. No throwing. No dumping. I can't wait to see how much fun you have."

She played for 45 more minutes without incident. Firm, clear, and consistent boundaries for the win.

TIPS FOR TABIES

Just like with all things, there are exceptions to rules. With sensory bins and tabies, we make a few exceptions as our tiniest littles are just learning to navigate life.

I started sensory bins with my youngest before his first birthday. I chose items he had eaten before (so they were allergy tested as safe for him) and items that did not pose a choking hazard. I kept it taste-safe and edible.

By the time he began talking, my son's third word (after Dada and Mama) was "Bin! Bin!" He would often bring me the blanket we used during sensory play like a dog with a leash. "Bin! Bin!" He loved sensory time so much.

Look at this little 12-month-old sensory bin-er!

As a taby, sensory bins were a blessing. They were an activity—a toy—that he could be successful with. His time as a taby was very frustrating and he was upset by his lack of "big kid status." Even though he needed an adult sitting next to him while he played, this was still nicer than trying to occupy his time as he bounced all over the house, angry about all that he couldn't do. He felt successful at a sensory bin and that feeling was worth every vacuumed up piece of rice.

Remember that with tabies (and all kids), parental supervision is a must. Use discretion for what is safe for your child and home. Reach out to your pediatrician if you have any questions about your child's safety with an activity.

- Tabies will still taste the world and that's OK. Use taste-safe items that are not a choking hazard and discourage licking, but don't freak out or make this a reason to NOT do sensory bins. Instead you can say, "Eww. Yucky. Don't eat this rice." If the sensory bin turns into an all-you-can-eat-buffet, that's when I take it away. I have found that doing sensory bins with tabies after a meal is better because they aren't hungry anymore. They're less likely to try and make the bin a meal.

- Tabies might try to dump or throw materials because they have very little impulse control. Stay really close to them and try to stop them before they dump or throw. You know the difference as a parent between an errant cup pour or "oops, I missed the bin" versus "I'm now going to redecorate the living room in rice." If things get excessive, remove the bin and let them know we are all done for today. No need to make a big deal out of it.

- The more a taby does a sensory bin, the less they eat and dump it. Even tabies understand rules and can follow them, but you have to work a little harder and be a little more understanding as they learn. They also grow in their knowledge of the items being played with ("Oh! I tasted this last time. It wasn't delicious. I'm not going to eat it.") Once they transition to toddlers, enforce the rules with more vigilance because by then they do know better. You'll know when to make that transition with your child—it'll be a gradual process.

- So much of sensory bins with tabies comes back to us as parents. Decide to start sensory bins when you are ready, on a day when you feel up to modeling and managing. Make sure to set yourself up for success. Have small goals and reasonable expectations—five minutes of play is huge for tabies, and they'll only get better from there.

TAKEAWAY MESSAGE

Sensory bins really are amazing, both for the kids who play with them and the parents who supervise them. Some of the most amazing skills my kids have learned (and that I learned as a parent) happened while sitting around a storage container full of rice.

17

SENSORY BIN ACTIVITIES

Sensory bins start with two supplies: the container and the base. These aren't complicated or fancy setups, and just those two supplies begin all the fun. From there, add tools or toys for your child to interact and engage with.

Here's a quick list of sensory bin supplies. You don't need to own everything on this list. A little goes a long way in the world of sensory (but PS: you probably already have most of this).

- Storage bin (I prefer a 28 quart or 41 quart bin)
- Blanket or towel
- The base (see list of bases)
- Measuring cups
- Funnels
- Muffin tin
- Ice cube tray
- Plastic bowls
- Plastic cups

WARNING

All activities need to be done under direct adult supervision. Use discretion for what is safe for your child and home. Reach out to your pediatrician if you have any questions about your child's safety with an activity.

SENSORY BIN BASES

Sensory bin bases are divided into two categories: taste-safe and not taste-safe. For younger children or children who are more likely to lick or try to eat some of the sensory material, pick from the taste-safe list. Taste-safe items are edible and less likely to be choked on. Older children who are not likely to try to eat the sensory material can, at your discretion, try items from the not taste-safe list. Not taste-safe items are not edible and may pose a choking hazard. Reach out to your pediatrician if you have any questions about the safety of items on either of these lists.

Many of the items that are dry or uncooked can be reused. Store materials like rice, beans, cornmeal, oats, and pasta in plastic bags or airtight containers for years of play.

THE TASTE-SAFE LIST

- Uncooked rice
- Cooked spaghetti
- Cereal
- Water
- Cornmeal
- Crushed ice
- Jell-O
- Pudding
- Gloop
- Whipped cream
- Dry oats

THE NOT TASTE-SAFE LIST

- Dried beans
- Pom-pom balls
- Water beads
- Ice cubes
- Dried chickpeas
- Mud
- Bubbles
- Slime
- Uncooked pasta
- Shredded paper
- Shaving cream

RICE BIN

SUPPLIES

- Uncooked rice
- Storage bin
- Various kitchen utensils

HOW-TO

Pour all the rice in the bin and add random kitchen utensils (such as measuring cups, scoops, and bowls).

WHY IT'S GOOD

It's a sensory bin! Besides that, rice is awesome for teaching kids about capacity and cause and effect as they experiment with different pouring techniques.

WHAT ELSE

The rice bin is a blank canvas. Add in toys, use recycled items like egg cartons, try muffin tins or ice cube trays, and even try hiding pieces of chunky puzzles underneath.

You can save the rice in a plastic bag or airtight container.

POURING STATION

SUPPLIES

- Two storage bins
- Measuring cups
- Funnels
- Ice cube tray
- Water
- Food coloring (optional)

HOW-TO

Set the larger bin on a towel. Fill a smaller bin with water and place it inside the larger empty bin. You can add a drop of food coloring, but that's optional. Set up a variety of supplies for your child to pour water into.

WHY IT'S GOOD

Pouring is a life skill. Children can't learn to pour without practice. This is a low-stakes way to teach the skill without orange juice spilling all over the kitchen floor (because how fun is that to clean up …).

WHAT ELSE

Pouring water is fun! Whenever your child "runs out of water," carefully pick up the larger bin and pour the water back into the smaller bin. It doesn't get old.

SHREDDED PAPER DINOSAUR BIN

SUPPLIES

- Shredded paper
- Toy dinosaurs
- Large storage bin

HOW-TO

Pour all the shredded paper into the large bin and add in dinosaurs (or other toys just dying to play in this bin).

WHY IT'S GOOD

It's unexpected and magical. The texture of the paper makes for a different kind of sensory experience.

WHAT ELSE

Full disclosure—this is one of the messiest bins, but it vacuums up in a hot second. The 90 minutes my kids played with it was well worth the 5 minutes of vacuuming (that my carpet needed anyway).

OATMEAL BIN

SUPPLIES

- Container of oats
- Storage bin
- Kitchen utensils

HOW-TO

Pour the oats into the bin. Add in a variety of utensils and let your child's imagination take the lead.

WHY IT'S GOOD

Oats are a great, taste-safe material that move in a fun way. Kids will learn cause and effect, capacity, scooping, pouring, and measuring skills.

WHAT ELSE

The very first time my toddler got to play with oatmeal, he declared it, "the best bin ever!" Now there's a winning review.

You can save the oats in a plastic bag or airtight container.

SCOOPING & SPOONING

SUPPLIES

- Storage bin
- Empty egg carton
- Scoop or spoon
- Cornmeal

HOW-TO

Pour cornmeal into the bin and add an egg carton along with a scoop or spoon. Show your child how to use the scoop to fill each section of the egg carton.

WHY IT'S GOOD

Kids learn skills through experiences and this activity is full of them. It teaches children how to use a spoon and how to transfer materials, both of which are lifelong skills.

WHAT ELSE

Try varying the spoons for this activity—for example, use a soup spoon, formula scoop, and mixing spoon. Switch from an egg carton to bowls, from cornmeal to rice. It won't be repetitive for a child.

You can save the cornmeal or rice in a plastic bag or airtight container.

TOY WATER RESCUE

SUPPLIES

- Favorite plastic toys (water-safe)
- Two storage bins
- Slotted spoon
- Food coloring (optional)
- Water

HOW-TO

Fill the smaller bin with water, add a drop of food coloring (optional), and toss in a ton of your child's favorite plastic toys. Set that bin inside the larger bin. Give your child a slotted spoon and have them rescue the toys from the water into the empty bin.

WHY IT'S GOOD

This activity gives children a chance to use their arm and hand muscles as well as grip strength to maneuver the slotted spoon through the water. It takes a lot of hand-eye coordination, problem-solving, and planning to rescue the toys.

WHAT ELSE

This activity can be done again and again by varying the toys to be rescued. Try themes such as cars, animals, and TV characters.

CLEAN THE CARS

SUPPLIES

- Two storage bins
- Mud
- Toy cars
- Soapy water
- Scrubbing brushes

HOW-TO

Fill the smaller bin with soapy water (use a tear-free soap). In the larger bin, add dirt from the yard and water to create mud. Toss in toy cars that are safe to get wet. Let your kids clean the now muddy cars.

WHY IT'S GOOD

Not only does this activity promote sensory play with mud and water, it gives children a clear purpose: clean the cars. Working independently to achieve a goal is an important life skill for kids to grow and develop.

WHAT ELSE

Use this basic setup to clean all sorts of outdoor toys: construction vehicles, plastic animals, and gardening tools. Kids love cleaning their muddy toys.

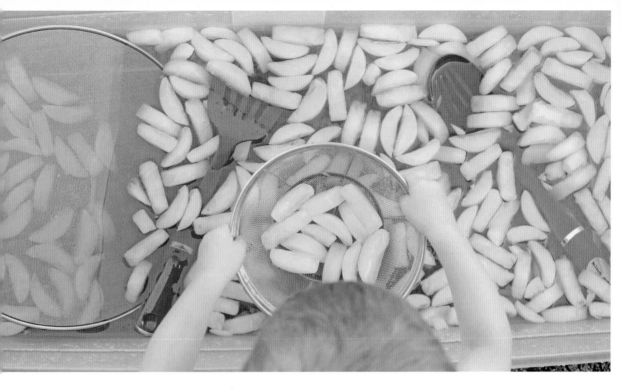

ICE BIN

SUPPLIES

- Storage bin
- Ice cubes
- Various kitchen utensils
- Food coloring (optional)

HOW-TO

Add several scoops of ice cubes to a sensory bin. Then add a little bit of water, food coloring (optional), and provide some kitchen utensils to play with. Let your child experiment with touching the ice for a chilly sensory experience.

WHY IT'S GOOD

This activity is great for using so many senses. The sound the ice cubes make in the bin as they clang around is especially inviting. Make sure to talk about any changes to the ice cubes during play (melting).

WHAT ELSE

Remember, large ice cubes are a choking hazard. Stay close to your child while they play and avoid whole ice cubes for kids who are likely to try and eat one.

FOAM BATH

SUPPLIES

- Tear-free soap
- Water
- Electric mixer
- Food coloring (optional)
- Various bowls and other kitchen utensils

HOW-TO

In a large bowl, combine 2 cups water with ½ cup tear-free soap (add in a few drops of food coloring if desired). Blend on high with a stand or hand mixer until stiff peaks form. Repeat for additional colors. Place your child in a bath tub with the foam and provide some kitchen utensils for them to play with.

WHY IT'S GOOD

This is such a fun sensory activity for kids and is a great indoor or outdoor activity. Foam is almost magical for kids. It's fluffy fun!

WHAT ELSE

In a bath tub, this activity is very slippery. Kids will need to stay seated the entire time.

18

MAKE SURVIVAL MODE YOUR BFF

I had no idea what "survival mode" was when this photo was taken, but eventually, I learned . . .

I decided one night to make dinner . . . (I'm guessing we all know it didn't go well because why would I tell you about my culinary win in a parenting book?)

I decided at eight weeks postpartum, with a newborn and a 21-month-old, and a life that felt completely upside down, that I was going to make dinner. Not just any dinner, but a new recipe. Duh. Can't make this easy on myself!

I felt like my family needed me back.

I wasn't being the mom I had been.

I wasn't being the wife I had been.

I didn't feel like the same person I had been just a few weeks before. I felt this need to get back on track and have our normal life again. I was, of course, 100% wrong in this feeling, but we'll get to that. Hold tight.

Shocker: the dinner was a disaster. Like a metaphor for everything I was feeling.

About the time the dinner was burning, the newborn was screaming and my taby was pulling every utensil out of the drawers in an effort to help (I think) what even he recognized as a sinking ship . . . that's when I dropped my phone in the dirty sink water.

Even through all the tears, I remembered that hack about the rice. Toss the phone in the rice to dry it out.

So I grabbed a bag of rice, ripped it open, dropped in my phone, and hung my head in shame, sadness, and complete defeat.

I sat on the floor and cried with a 21-month-old comforting me.

"It OK, Mommy. It OK."

But it didn't feel OK.

I felt so far away from where I was supposed to be—and might I add, this dinner idea was just something I had decided. No one was telling me to do it. But I was feeling all this internal pressure. All the guilt. All the expectations to "bounce back" and get things going again. There was just no way I could do that yet.

I didn't call my mom that night because I knew I'd just start crying on the phone. But when I saw her next, I made a passing statement to test the waters—because I didn't want to come out and say, "I'm drowning," which is exactly what I should have said.

I said something like, "Man, at least Daniel Tiger has a good mom because she's basically the one raising Sam right now since I'm always with the baby."

Sam in action—pulling out the utensils and covering them in cheese. The last photo my phone took before I dropped it.

And without missing a beat, my mom (who parented in a much different, much more guilt-free time than I am) replied with: "Whatever! You're in survival mode right now. Do what you have to do to survive."

That was literally all she said and my whole world changed.

I was in survival mode. Maybe I can do this after all.

Since that day in 2015, when the dinner burned and the world collapsed and I realized it was OK to pause and take a beat on normal life for a while, I've learned a lot about survival mode. My mom was right (she pretty much always is).

> **Survival mode doesn't mean you've given up on life and this is what it is. It means giving yourself a whole lot of grace to go through a really hard time.**

So. Much. Grace.

Parenting won't look the same in survival mode as it did before. That's OK. You'll get back on track.

Home life won't look the same in survival mode and that's OK too. You'll vacuum again another time.

The world invented boxed mac and cheese and DVDs because survival mode was meant to exist.

The problem is . . . well, you know what the problem is. It's the pressure and the expectation of what we perceive as right and a lot of that comes from social media. It's a hard time to be a parent.

The bottom line is to cut yourself some slack when you're going through something major or going through a big transition. Remember that this isn't forever, this is just survival mode until you can get back on your feet. And you will get there.

Give yourself a lot of grace. Weather the storm. Don't try to erase it or speed it up. It really is OK for things to not be OK.

At some point, and I don't know when that will be, the clouds will part and the sun will shine and you will breathe again. You'll turn off the TV. Parenting will be exactly as you remember it, and you'll start walking forward.

Until then, take all the grace you need.

Just like my son said to me, "It'll be OK." I promise.

TIMES I'VE GONE INTO SURVIVAL MODE:

- During morning sickness
- The end of a pregnancy
- Through postpartum
- When we remodeled our kitchen
- As my husband finished his MBA
- When it took nine months to remodel the rest of the house
- Anytime I'm sick or two of three kids are sick
- During a global pandemic
- While I was writing this book (wink)

EPILOGUE FROM MY BURNED DINNER

My 21-month-old was right. It really did end up being OK.

My husband came home that night with Happy Meals and a big hug, laughing at the mess I'd made trying to impress basically only myself.

My phone dried out a few days later and turned back on—the trick worked! But I was left with a seemingly useless bag of now dirty rice.

I remembered vaguely an idea that you can put rice in a bin for kids to play with and that it was supposed to be really fun. I even kind of remembered a cornmeal table in the church basement when I was a kid.

I found an old under-the-bed storage bin we'd had since college, dumped out the junk we didn't need, and poured the rice in there. I added some kitchen utensils to be fancy.

The actual photo of my very first sensory bin.

That was the first sensory bin I ever made, and four months later, I opened an Instagram account called Busy Toddler. My whole existence changed and it ended up more than OK.

TAKEAWAY MESSAGE

Tell all your friends about survival mode. Welcome them into it, encourage them to hold their heads high, and to never be ashamed of walking a rough road. The more we can normalize survival mode, the more we can let off a lot of the unnecessary pressure and expectations of parenting.

19

SITTERVISING

Sittervise (sit·ter·vise) verb
Supervise from a seated position.

In my humblest opinion, sittervising is the pinnacle of parenting. Anytime I have a brief moment to sittervise my children instead of following them around (or rather, have them follow me around), I hear angels singing.

It's a glorious occasion in parenting when you get the chance to start sittervising—it just happens all of a sudden, out of thin air.

One day, you'll go from helping them up every twist and turn at a park, managing their safety, and making sure the ladder isn't too high . . . to *sitting on the park bench.*

But will you make the decision to sit?

Sittervising a sensory bin with my toddler playing, the baby napping, and my coffee mostly hot. Living the dream.

So many parents in our generation choose to keep standing and following their children far longer than needed, when sittervising would do just fine. The protective instincts kick in and the fear of "what if" takes over our adult minds.

But remember, our job is to make sure kids have the skills to stand on their own two feet and become self-sufficient adults. We need to teach them through their own practice to handle play (and life!) on their own.

They can't do that if we are right behind them waiting, insinuating we know they will fall and fail, or hovering and questioning their every move. They'll never develop that natural ability to weigh the risk on their own.

Sittervising is a great chance for you to watch your child play and watch them navigate the world with you on the sidelines. You're still a featured player and still on safety watch, but you're doing it from the bench and trusting your child to make some great judgment calls too.

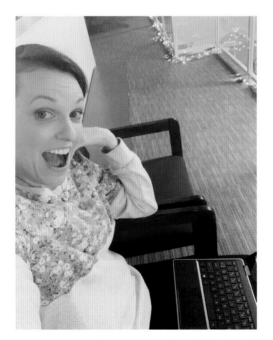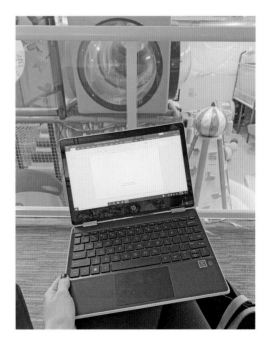

I was even occasionally sittervising the kids at a play place while editing this book.

Sittervising outdoor play from the warmth of my kitchen.

After all, it's their body and they do know what they're comfortable with.

There are so many skills our kids need to learn in early childhood and one of the greatest skills is risk management. They do that best when we are sitting. They need the chance to make their own decisions and possibly their own mistakes, because that is when real learning happens.

We need to take this chance in early childhood to let our children get used to managing life on their own (under our watch but minus the hovering), because there will come a time in the distant (but all too near) future when we'll be left sitting at home far from the action.

What happens to the child who never got a chance to practice their risk management skills, but then is thrust into middle school on their own? Little chances we have to give kids some autonomy and let them safely explore the world—these add up over time.

So, take a load off and do some sittervising when you realize you've reached this moment. It may seem like you aren't doing much, but you're actually making a really great parenting move by letting your child move on their own.

BE SMART ABOUT SITTERVISING

I'm not advocating against supervising children or letting them into unsafe situations in the name of learning risk management. Make sure an area is safe for your child. Make sure an area is appropriate for them and their skills. Make sure the environment and the choices your child will be faced with are in your comfort zone. Be present, be alert, and use good judgment as you supervise your child.

20

SICK DAY ACTIVITIES

Let's be frank: the sick leave policy for the job of parenting is a joke and we've got to form a union. They can't treat us this way! I demand sick days. While we negotiate this contract, we also might want to talk about overtime, job-related injury, and vacation pay. The work conditions for parenting are really subpar.

There's nothing harder than trying to parent a young child when you are sick. It's a misery you can only really appreciate when you get there.

We want to sit.

We want to binge watch all the TV.

We want someone to be our parent for the day and make us chicken noodle soup.

But it's not going to happen.

I always bust out an activity for my kids that I can sit and watch them do—as funny as that sounds, because why add MORE work to these sick days?! But it's a few seconds of work that gives me a whole lot of minutes to rest and watch and maybe not answer any "but why" questions while I'm feeling crummy.

It works like a charm and for at least a few minutes (or often longer with these activities), I can lie down or crumple into the couch . . . or heck, the bathroom floor, and actually feel like I'm getting a tiny bit of rest.

In honor of parent sick days, here are some of my favorite "sit and watch" activities that don't take much sickness energy to set up, but will occupy our kids while we attempt to get well.

WARNING

All activities need to be done under direct adult supervision. Use discretion for what is safe for your child and home. Reach out to your pediatrician if you have any questions about your child's safety with an activity.

POPSICLE BATH

SUPPLIES

- Popsicle
- Bathtub

HOW-TO

This is as simple as it sounds: a toddler taking a bath while eating a Popsicle. Fill the bathtub just as you normally would. Set your toddler in the bathtub and hand them a Popsicle (or any ice pop) to enjoy as they bathe. Now you can enjoy sitting and relaxing for many minutes as you sittervise. Once done, clean your toddler like normal and revel in their happiness.

WHY IT'S GOOD

The Popsicle bath is the real hero of kids' activities. Everyone comes out a winner. It's also a serious sensory activity with the juxtaposition of the warm water versus the cold Popsicle.

WHAT ELSE

This activity will forever be the greatest reset button in parenting. Sick kids? Sick mom? Mad kids? Mad dad? Popsicle bath. It changes everything.

CRAYON DROP

SUPPLIES

- Recycled container (oats or sour cream containers work great)
- Knife (for prep and adult use ONLY)
- Crayons

HOW-TO

Start by cutting three small holes into the lid. Make the slit large enough to fit each crayon. Once the crayon can fit through the hole, rub the crayon in and out of the hole to help make it the right size. Once your child finishes pushing all the crayons through the slot, show them how to take the lid off and begin the activity again.

WHY IT'S GOOD

It's a fine motor skills activity that's also full of spatial awareness (to orient the crayons vertically) and hand-eye coordination. This activity requires lots of concentration.

WHAT ELSE

Don't have crayons? Try paper straws, craft sticks, or toothpicks instead.

BRICK BATH

SUPPLIES

- Plastic building bricks
- Bathtub

HOW-TO

Fill the bathtub like you normally would for your toddler, BUT spice it up by dumping in lots of plastic building bricks. Let your kiddo build in the water for as long as they want (our record was an hour-long brick bath and three times adding in more hot water).

When your toddler is done, use a colander to scoop out the bricks and lay them on a towel to dry. Make sure the bricks are separated and the studs are right side up to drain the water out. That's a great job for little hands to take care of. I've never had any problem with mold—my bricks always come out much cleaner than before.

WHY IT'S GOOD

It's a chance for your child to build in water and experience all of the fun STEM challenges that come with that. It's also a great sensory experience to be immersed in a bathtub full of plastic building bricks.

WHAT ELSE

Think of all the bath plus toys possibilities out there. Any toy that is sealed and plastic will work great, like toy cars or plastic dolls.

PILLOW FLOOR LAVA

SUPPLIES

- All the pillows
- All the cushions
- All the blankets

HOW-TO

Together with your child, cover the floor of a single room with every pillow, couch cushion, and blanket you can find. Let your child bounce, play, and create stories in this wacky-floor environment.

WHY IT'S GOOD

This is a crazy-good gross motor skill activity. It has kids using their whole body and balance skills to walk through the uneven terrain.

WHAT ELSE

Don't pull all the pillows down—leave ONE couch intact to lie on and sittervise as your child explores the pillow land.

HUNT AND FIND

SUPPLIES

- Half sheets of construction paper
- Marker
- Painter's tape

HOW-TO

Cut a bunch of sheets of construction paper in half. On those sheets, write out letters, numbers, shapes, or simple words—pick the focus that is right for your child. You can also leave the half sheets blank to be a color finding activity. Tape these sheets around the room and sit or lie on the couch. Yell out what your child should go find and how to find it: "RUN to the letter M!" "Hop to the word *and*." "Jump to the color red!" "Crawl to the square" and so on.

WHY IT'S GOOD

This activity gets kids MOVING. It helps them to actively engage and learn using their whole body.

WHAT ELSE

Try varying your calls: "Jump to the word that rhymes with cat." "Bounce to the letter that says mmmm." "Run to the shape of a piece of pizza."

ERASE THE ABCs

SUPPLIES

- Window or glass door
- Dry-erase marker
- Towel

HOW-TO

On your window or a sliding glass door, write the letters of the alphabet in a mixed-up order. You can lie on the couch or sit in a chair while calling out which letter to erase (one by one).

WHY IT'S GOOD

This activity packs in a lot of goodness: it gives children a chance to play with the ABCs, promotes visual discrimination skills, and lets kids build arm strength by working with a vertical surface.

WHAT ELSE

Consider varying this activity (for example, with numbers, shapes, words, and math problems) to fit the child. Also, try changing the way you call out letters: "This letter says *wwww*." Or: "I hear this letter at the start of *man*."

21

THE WONDERFUL WORLD OF SIBLINGS

Still to date, my favorite photo of pal Sam (15 months old) and me.

Oh Em Gee! Your "baby" is going to become a big sibling. The party is about to start.

> **Pro tip: Once the new baby is born, bring home their cap from the hospital for your child to sniff and become better acquainted with the smells of the new sibling.**

WAIT. That's from my dog parenting book.

Scratch that; let's start over.

Sibling relationships are amazing.

These people will have each other their entire lives—and if making sure they grow up liking each other isn't a daunting task, I don't know what is. Talk about a nine on the pressure scale.

Going from one child to having siblings brings on a whole new world of parenting to explore. You once had time to craft the entire day around a baby's schedule, but now you have another child's life to juggle, while creating a safe space for the new baby to grow. Oh and don't forget, you're running on less sleep and holding up more balls in the air than you ever thought possible. This feels great and not at all overwhelming (so much sarcasm).

The added task of not only raising multiple children, but raising those kids to be loving siblings—holy moly. Things just got real.

But don't worry, it'll be OK. There are ways, there are tools, and I've got more than a few tricks to help you navigate this sibling world.

> **Helping siblings become friends might be one of the most important jobs we have as parents, and it's a job I take really seriously.**

I HAD TWO UNDER TWO, AND THEN THREE IN THREE YEARS

I knew what I looked like buckling up my barely 3-year-old and not even 18-month-old into the car. I knew how I looked reaching and stretching over my clearly third-trimester belly. I knew what eyes rolling sounded like.

We were finished at the grocery store and getting ready to head home. I was answering 47 toddler questions about snacks, and could we watch yet another episode of their favorite cartoon (probably), and did we have to wear shoes in the car (I guess not?) when I noticed another mom watching us intently.

She was about 15 years older than me with a black jacket and a purple scarf. Her hair was a mix of blonde and gray, starting to lean more to the latter. I remember exactly what she looked like.

Eventually, she started walking over. I bristled slightly, instinctively, knowing what would come next. Twenty-eight weeks of being pregnant with my third child in three years and

I knew exactly what she was going to say.

But which condescending comment would it be?

- Boy, you've got your hands full.

- Was this planned?

- Why have another? You already have one of each!

- Having that baby is going to be so much more work. It's so hard to have three.

- Three kids is the worst! Better to just have four.

- Those first few years were a nightmare for us. Good luck . . .

I'd heard them all and then some, and I usually just smiled and nodded and got the heck out of there.

But what she actually said stopped me in my tracks.

What things looked like around here before we added Baby 3 (Matt) to the party.

Instead of spewing judgment or peppering me with warnings of bad days to come, this mom said something I had waited two trimesters to hear.

I wish I had hugged her.

I wish now, years later, that I could tell her how much what she said meant to me. And how true it was.

She gently touched my shoulder to get my attention, and as I turned, I saw she was smiling from ear to ear, and she had such kindness in her eyes.

Living my best two under two life back in the day.

"We had three kids in under four years and it was the best thing ever. You're going to have so much fun."

That's it. That's all she said and it was like the world slowed around us and I could breathe again. If I wasn't mid-buckle, wedged into the car, belly half smashed, I would have jumped out and hugged her.

Thank you for not judging me.

Thank you for not feeling like I needed a lecture.

Thank you for spreading kind words that are encouraging to a new parent, not terrifying.

It made me so aware of the words I say to families and to make sure that I share the positives. We all know there are pluses and minuses with any way we structure our families. We don't need to be warned about all the negatives, because frankly, that won't make one bit of difference . . . and they might not come true.

Did I need anyone to tell me three kids was going to be insane? NO! I knew that. I didn't need anyone telling me "just you wait" as if some cloud of misery was about to rain on my parade. I didn't need to hear those things.

My 3 in 3 years: 20 months old, newborn, 3 years old. What a party!

I needed to hear happiness. I needed to hear joy. I needed to hear the same excitement for this baby as everyone seemed to have when it was my first.

I'd heard all the negative comments two years earlier when we were embarking on two kids under two.

The whole previous pregnancy was full of poorly timed negative comments from others about what a struggle we were about to encounter. The joke was on them, because they were all wrong.

Two under two wasn't a crazy, insurmountable struggle. I loved it.

I loved having two under two.

I loved it so much, I decided to do two under two again with a three-year-old kicker.

It worked *for me.*

So, here's my brief open letter to expecting families about to enter the world of two under two, or the parents freshly home with a newborn and a toddler in tow, or the couples wondering if having kids so close together will be OK.

Dear Parents,

Two under two was a joy. It was a fun party and a quick ride and I loved it. Loved it enough to get on the ride again.

There will be hard days. But that's what life is like whether your kids are 10 months apart or 10 years apart. This isn't some exclusive problem for the #twoundertwo hashtag.

There will be magical days when you can't imagine life without or before these beautiful babies.

There will be hectic, trying, amazing, wonderful, crazy, insane, and lovely days, but again—that's not a two under two thing. That's a "having kids" thing. And then there will be a moment when life becomes normal again, the routine returns, and you'll be the parent effortlessly juggling two kids in the store parking lot without breaking a sweat.

And maybe you'll see a pregnant person holding a toddler's hand, staring at you in awe.

I hope you'll lift them up and set them in a good place. Tell them it's going to be fine. That it's going to be great. That it will be the best ride of their life and that you couldn't be happier or more excited for them.

Share the best parts of this adventure. Share the kind words you needed to hear.

At the very least, we can spread encouragement to new families, not fear, and stop the cycles of negativity. Because while there are some hectic days in any family, we don't need to scare people out of parenthood just because of a few bad days. We can spread kindness.

Consider the words you say to future parents. Consider what you wish someone would have said to you. Make the world a better place for parents joining the club.

The beginning of them as a three-some. The Kid Team.

THE SIBLING RELATIONSHIP REALLY IS A TREASURE

We hear the words *siblings* and *parenting* books and the automatic space we go to is fighting, trouble sharing, tattling, and jealousy. In other words: negative, negative, negative.

Yes, those things happen with siblings and we have to tackle all those domains, but honestly, who wouldn't fight with a permanent roommate they didn't choose? It's like a blind date taken to the nth degree.

As parents, we often think our job is to referee the sibling relationship and to act as the mediator or the negotiator between two sides in an epic conflict. To just keep the peace and keep them from destroying each other and the house.

I see it a little differently.

My job is to cultivate this relationship.

I want to help it grow, flourish, and be deeply rooted to stand the test of time. Siblings should be friends they never outgrow—so how can we make sure of this?

> **I'm asking us to refocus our ideas of siblings and remember that when the dust settles, this is the person they are left (hopefully) standing next to and loving deeply.**

If I can uphold true friendship as the main goal—not just tolerating each other and minimizing conflict—then I will have accomplished something truly great. This isn't an overnight thing. We are playing the long game here.

I've shifted my focus in two ways to help my kids grow in their relationship with each other. I'm going to say this very clearly without beating around the bush: this is what has worked for my family and what has helped my kids. Just for fun, let's say it one more time: this is what's working for my family. You know what's best for yours.

Our sibling team: bravely facing the world (and errands with mom) together.

HONOR THE SIBLING YEARS

I see so much value in the sibling relationship in early childhood. I know my kids have a lifetime of *their friends* and *my friends* in the future, so I view the early years as the sibling years.

The majority of their lives will be spent with other kids and other friends. To balance that, I made sure my kids had a solid foundation with their siblings. Rather than focusing on other social groups for my kids, I focused our family inward. The first and strongest friend group my kids have is their siblings. I did this intentionally and with purpose.

If there is a choice between signing up my kids for a separate activity versus them spending time together, I'll choose them spending time together. They'll have a lifetime of activities with other people. This is my *best shot* at fostering togetherness.

For me, when thinking about my children's need for recreational soccer at age three (although that looks fun), it pales in comparison to their need for sibling friendship and the time it takes to play and develop that connection.

Their relationship needs attention and opportunity, and if all my time is spent pulling them in different directions or driving them to different events, they miss out on time together. They will miss out on the chance to build a solid foundation together before the outside influences of other friends and their own independent lives begin.

Once they start school and start living their lives more independently, things will change. That's why, in these early years, I made a conscious choice to dedicate as much time as possible to sibling play.

While other activities will have their moment in the future, I'm prioritizing sibling time as the most valuable time. I believe with all my heart that investing in this time now will bring a far greater return for my kids. I treasure these sibling years—they are few and fleeting and priceless.

RESPECT EACH SIBLING IN THE FRIEND GROUP

It's very easy as a parent to shuffle younger siblings behind the oldest child—maybe pulling them to the older child's event or finding things to occupy them while waiting to pick up the big kid.

For me, this didn't work.

I didn't want my oldest to seem more special or more important or have more opportunities than my younger children just because he came first. I wanted to level the playing field. During these all-important sibling years, I didn't want to place the focus on one child or the other. I wanted to view them as a single unit, a kid team.

In our family, each child's ideas, thoughts, and time are valued. We do our best to respect the group and keep things fairly even. My husband and I refer to our kids as a unit, a team, a group, and we treat them as such.

Times will change as my kids age and they enter elementary school. They will start to form other interests and find other friends and join other activities. I have them all together as a kid team for such a small period of time, so it's a joy to give them as much time as possible to get to know one another without having to rush off to events or pickups or games.

The easiest ingredient is time.

Kids can't form a relationship with any friend unless they spend time with that person. The same goes for siblings. If we want our children to consider each other friends, we need to make time for them to do that.

It might mean saying no to some activities. You will have to prioritize time and their relationship, which means shifting your perspective and seeing them as a friend group.

We can help siblings develop deep, close bonds, but we must be intentional about it. This doesn't happen by accident. It happens when we make the sibling years a significant and sacred focus of our family.

ACTIVITIES ARE EXPENSIVE

I'm not over here trying to rag on kid soccer or ballet classes, but I am here to offer a different opinion. Part of my choice to keep the kids out of sports and classes was financial. It is very expensive to have three kids taking multiple classes for multiple years. What seems easy with one child gets more complicated with two or three or more. Considering the long-term financial commitment of these activities also weighed heavily on our decision to postpone signing up—especially when nurturing the lifelong sibling relationship is free. You are not limiting your child or holding them back by skipping early childhood sports, classes, or clubs.

22

HOW TO USE KID FIGHTS FOR GOOD

People fight. Friends fight. Roommates fight. Married couples fight. Little kids don't have the market cornered on this, although sometimes it feels like they've taken a bickering course at the local community college because they're so darn good at it.

All relationships have fights. The difference between kid fights (whether with siblings or friends) and other fights is . . . actually there are two key differences:

1. You have two YOUNG and NEW people with YOUNG and NEW minds that are not fully equipped with all the emotional maturity adults have. Each child on their own has trouble self-regulating and now they're left in a space full of potential objects to disagree over with another person who is learning interpersonal skills as well. Game on.

2. These fights are teachable moments because how a child learns to deal with conflict at this stage in life will have a direct impact on how they deal with it in the future. Every fight is a chance for each child to learn a new conflict resolution skill.

> **We must shift our perspective and see childhood arguments (both with friends and with siblings) as an opportunity to teach.**

It might be hard to do while Child A is yanking a toy from the hands of Child B, but try (*keyword here is try*) to shift your thinking—instead of seeing it as yet another fight, reframe it in your head as *yet another chance to help them learn*.

This is yet another chance to help them learn how to solve problems.

This is yet another chance to model conflict resolution strategies.

Frustrating when kids fight? YEAH. Totally frustrating.

But is it actually a thing that we can use for good? You bet it is.

If I have to choose between my kids fighting at home with me there to teach them about conflict resolution versus them being awful to a kid at school without me there to help, I'll always choose the option that I can turn into a teachable moment. I live for these moments.

Parenting is a giant game of chess with intricate moves and shifts. So much of it depends on our own perspective. We can't directly change what our children are doing (they are their own people), but we can change our way of thinking—and by doing so, we can have an indirect positive influence on them.

Shift your perspective on fights. Fights in early childhood are your best chance to directly teach and model conflict resolution skills for your children to use when you aren't around. These fights can actually do a lot of good.

PHRASES TO USE WHEN PEACEFUL PLAY BREAKS DOWN

There's nothing more fun than being midway through prepping dinner, hands covered in chicken guts, oil in a pan, and hearing the familiar shrill of a kid fight brewing. As the voices escalate, you can hear the sounds of imminent battle.

It makes your blood boil as a parent.

We're so much older and so much wiser. We know it doesn't matter who has the red train versus the blue train, but *it matters to the kids and they aren't as mature as we are*. Remember, you are dealing with two people who have limited to no conflict resolution skills or self-control (think back to the section on tantrums—Chapter 11—these fights have a lot in common with tantrums).

> **Fights will happen until our kids learn (from us) skills to handle tough situations. We can't expect our children to magically be born with conflict resolution skills. They need to be explicitly taught. And they need to be taught by us.**

Remember, I'm an educator and had been helping children learn about conflict resolution for years before I had my own kids. Children need help learning these skills and I've honed my technique over the past 15 years as both a teacher and a parent. I use these strategies with my own children and with any child I'm put in charge of (whether that child was in my class or is a friend in my home).

Let's kick it off with two things I DON'T do when I hear a fight beginning:

1. I never start screaming along with them. We don't need more people yelling and it will only add to the problem. Kids have the market cornered on screaming and they don't need any encouragement to get louder. Screaming begets screaming.

2. I don't go running to intervene right away. I give them a moment and a chance to handle things with the tools they have or are learning to use. They need a little time to try working through the situation without an adult because it's the only way they'll learn for future moments *when I'm actually not around*.

My goal is to use these fights as a teachable moment for problem-solving and conflict resolution. Don't miss these moments just because you're irritated they started fighting yet again. I know I've missed some great moments because I couldn't take another scream.

MY BEST RESPONSES TO KID FIGHTS

After years of helping kids through conflicts and heated arguments, I've settled on two main (simple) ways to help defuse situations so we can get to those teachable moments. My goal with both strategies is to help slow down the anger, encourage problem-solving, and help children move on safely from the disagreement.

1. Do you need an adult?

When I hear things start to go bad, I usually holler into the room, "Do you need an adult?" I don't step into the room. I holler (yes, holler) from where they can't see me. This question lets the kids know I'm aware of the situation (I know all and see all) and they need to find a resolution quickly or THE ADULT IS COMING.

They don't want me to intervene and that's a united party line they can usually agree on. Typically, kids work really fast to try and solve the problem.

If things are really bad, one child will say, "Yes, we need help." That's my cue to enter the room and hear about the disagreement from all parties involved. We talk about what happened, possible solutions, and where to go from there. I model, discuss, and teach different problem-solving techniques or conflict resolution strategies (I'll share more of those in a few pages) so that next time, maybe they won't need an adult to help with this particular issue.

2. Hands on your heads!

If I hear the kids really losing it (maybe someone is getting physical or is a breath away from that), I state firmly: "Hands on your heads!"

Instinctively, kids stop and put their hands on their heads. This quick statement from me sort of brings my kids back to reality and pauses the argument. If they're fighting over a single item, it often causes that item to be released by both kids or at least the pressure taken off of it.

Then I say (more quietly and calmly), "Hands on your ears, hands on your shoulders, hands on your belly, hands on your knees, hands touching." This ends with them folding their own hands and has given everyone a chance to stop and breathe.

The situation immediately calms down enough that we can all talk about it. It's no different than teaching an adult to count to ten before reacting. It alleviates so much of the pressure that's building.

Again, we have an open discussion and work together to form a new game plan. Their involvement in problem-solving and conflict resolution is definitely dependent on the child and their age. At first, you'll need to take the lead and model it. Over time, kids get better at coming up with their own strategies and you'll see firsthand how your hard work is paying off.

But it is hard work. This isn't easy. The important stuff never is.

> **If a child doesn't like the end decision, I invite them to find a quiet space to sit and think, and I'll come touch base with them. This gives them a chance to be alone, decompress, and be heard individually. I'm available to help them with their feeling of disappointment.**

CONFLICT RESOLUTION STRATEGIES AND TRICKS TO TEACH KIDS

Matt: thrilled to share. Kate: not so excited.

As much as I'd love to live and be with my kids forever, that's not the path we're on and I need to get them ready for life outside our house. Part of life outside the home is dealing with conflict and disagreements with others.

We can't undervalue how important it is to help kids learn these skills now to use later in life.

I teach my kids specific strategies to use when they disagree with friends (whether that's siblings, cousins, neighbors or classmates) that they can use throughout their lives. Kids need help learning ways to handle and manage conflict or disagreements—they weren't born knowing this. The best way to teach these strategies is by modeling them AND explicitly teaching them. As my kids work through their conflicts with each other or with friends, my goal is for them to resolve the issue without needing adult help. Giving them strategies to try is the best way to work toward that goal (which will come, again, with age and maturity).

But when do we have time to teach these strategies to kids? There are two great times:

1. After having a conflict, we often talk about strategies to use or try. Here's what happened, here's what went well, here's what went not-so-well, and here's what you could try instead.

2. Another good time to talk about these strategies is in the car or at dinner—when emotions aren't flying high. Pose questions to talk about: "What would you do if your friend knocked over your block tower?" Generate some ideas and plant these seeds of conflict resolution techniques.

So much of parenting is being proactive and staying ahead of the curve. Teaching conflict resolution strategies BEFORE they've even had the conflict is huge.

Here are some phrases and strategies I teach my kids:

- **"I need a break" and "I'm having a hard time."** I teach these phrases to toddlers to help them vocalize their needs instead of going to Tantrum Land (see Chapter 11 on toddler tantrums). We also use these phrases in our home as generic codes to verbalize our feelings even beyond the toddler years. When I hear a child say these words, I immediately walk over, check in, and usually the other sibling comes too, so we can all have a quick conversation about how things are going.

- **Find another fun.** When kids realize their game plan or idea is no longer working, it's time to move on together. They say to each other, "Let's find another fun" and off they go. Not all games are going to work and it's OK to abandon ship all together.

- **Make a new plan.** This phrase is a great way to introduce compromise to little kids. When they say, "Let's make a new plan," they work to make sure each participant is happy.

- **Walk away.** I encourage my kids to walk away or leave a bad play situation. They are taught they don't need to stay and play in a game where they aren't comfortable. Often this mini-break is enough to reset the play clock.

These aren't fancy tools but they're useful, and it sure is magical when you hear a four-year-old say, "Let's make a new plan together" instead of hitting her brother with a dump truck. This can happen. But it doesn't happen by chance. It doesn't happen because I have magical unicorn kids or taught kids with pixie dust sprinkled everywhere. It happens by being involved, being proactive, and modeling conflict resolution skills. It happens by teaching.

Kids can learn to solve their own problems and we need to encourage this—because we want to raise independent kids. We do this by slowing our reaction time (give them a minute to work things out) and teaching them tools and strategies to help when disagreements arise. They won't learn these tools on their own. It is our privilege as parents to teach them.

THE FRIENDSHIP TRAIN

After a few hard days of nonstop sibling disagreements, I'd had enough. The kids needed reteaching. In a classroom, we know it's time to reteach a subject when skills have slipped or waned. The same goes for kids and their behaviors at home.

After a bad stretch of sibling fighting and a lapse in demonstrating good conflict resolution skills, along with a mom about done with the constant screeching, I pulled my kids together for some direct teaching in friendship strategies—but they didn't know that's what we were doing. They thought we were building a "friendship train."

I brought them into a room with all of our wooden trains and loads of other supplies. Together, we built a giant train and imaginary play world. I knew that fights and conflict would happen while they were building. I was actually counting on it.

Every time a conflict happened, I stopped the group dramatically. "I heard you yell at him for a curved piece. Next time, try 'Can you please hand me that piece?' Let's practice." "I see you're angry that piece won't fit. Tell us, 'I'm frustrated. I need help.'"

As we built the train track, we actively talked about friendship skills, strategies, phrases to use, and kindness. And it wasn't by accident.

I call it a friendship train because we work on friendship skills through intentional parenting. My kids think it's about making a train track with friends, which it is . . . but it's also a whole lot more.

THE RULE FOR SHARING

Sharing is hard for kids and a bit of predicament in early childhood.

On one hand, we want to raise children who notice others. We want our children to be generous . . . but that's a mess of abstract concepts that's really hard for someone with a new brain to handle.

Kids see in black and white. What's mine is mine and what's yours is also mine. It's really hard for them to understand ownership rules.

This is next level sharing (but still so cute).

Brothers.

It can feel a bit icky to force a child to share a toy they're using. If it's their personal toy, that would be like you having to share your phone half the time with a friend or stranger. It's not going to happen.

When we make a child give up a toy before they're done using it, it's like cutting off their stream of thought and interrupting a conversation. Play is hard work and it's complicated. We want to honor the work our child is doing with a toy and let them fully finish before we ask them to give it away.

But how can we help kids share?! They have to share at some point!!

You're right, they do! They have to learn to notice others, understand how to take turns, and be generous people. This will take time, age, growth, maturity, communication skills, and interpersonal skills. In other words: sharing is a really hard skill and it's OK that your two-year-old isn't great at it. They're really young and need years of sharing training before they've mastered the art.

So instead of ripping a toy from a playing child or forcing that child to give it up before they are ready, let's empower kids to make their needs known.

> **Here's the key phrase: "When you're done, can I have a turn?"**
>
> **Answer: "Yes, when I am done, you can have a turn."**

This works WONDERS with kids. They get it. It takes an abstract concept like sharing and puts it into very concrete terms: *When you are done with that, I'm next up for it.*

The child playing with the toy knows they don't have to give it up right away.

The child waiting for the toy knows they will get a turn eventually.

Let me tell you—from years of educating children and raising my kids—this phrase works. But you have to teach it. Remember, they don't know better. They aren't born knowing how to share or take social cues that someone is waiting for a toy. We have to directly model and explain how this interaction works.

We don't need to force sharing or take toys away. We can honor our kids and empower them to make these decisions and have these kinds of conversations. We can help them notice someone waiting to play and encourage them to remember that person wants the toy *when they're done.*

Someday, we won't be there to help them share or make sure they get a turn, so it's of the utmost important that we teach them these skills and phrases today.

THE RULE FOR TATTLING

Tattling is the worst.

It drives parents up the wall—and it's a childhood struggle that begins in the early years and lasts well into elementary school. UNLESS kids know "The Rule About Tattling."

I started this routine as a teacher, and I continue to apply it at home to my kids. When a child comes to me with a complaint about a sibling or another child, I break it down like this:

- Is someone hurt?

- Is someone in danger?

If the answer is NO, the child is simply looking to report another child for a rules infraction—or they are looking to report a behavior they personally didn't like. We all know which kids are very rule-oriented and get their feathers ruffled easily versus other kids who aren't that way. Trust me, I have one of each and then a third who kind of skates in both lanes.

No tattling here. Just three kids making some excellent choices together . . .

We want kids to both trust each other AND be on the lookout for each other, which is hard to do without some tattling creeping in. This is the reality of childhood and the reality of kids learning social norms and expectations. Your child is not abnormal for tattling.

Here's the conversation I've had with my kids (and students) about tattling—while they're playing nicely, NOT during a moment of tattling:

- If someone is hurt or in danger of getting hurt, PLEASE come tell me ASAP. No matter what—I need to know. Keeping kids safe is the most important job.

- If no one is hurt or about to get hurt, let it go. Maybe walk away. Maybe talk to them about it. You don't need to tell me things to get someone in trouble. That's not how things work around here.

And that's it. Simple as that.

It doesn't need to be some long, drawn-out conversation. Kids are smart. They understand the difference between a safety concern and "so-and-so used too much toilet paper and you should get mad at them." Even in the toddler years, they get the distinction.

This is what I say when a child is NOT tattling: "Oh my goodness, they are slamming doors upstairs! Thank you for letting me know about that safety concern." And off I go to stop it before someone loses a finger.

Here's what I say if they are tattling: "The other kids are playing with the pillows on the blue couch. Are they hurt? Are they in danger? Remember, we don't tattle on our friends to try and get them in trouble." End of discussion.

Kids are smart about tattling. If we enforce the tattling boundary and rule firmly and with consistency, it's an easy concept for them to grasp.

Side note: I will tell you, honestly, that after shooing away the tattler, if I find a complaint to be interesting and something I want to check out, I do a "mom walk-by" and see for myself. And if necessary, I intervene on my own terms.

TAKEAWAY MESSAGE

Kids will fight. This is what happens with new brains still learning self-control. Our job as parents is to lead, model, guide, teach, reteach, and help them find these skills. Remind yourself again and again: they are not born with these skills. They have to learn them from us.

23

FRIENDSHIP ACTIVITIES

A pouring station for three.

There's nothing like a good activity to bring kids together in play.

Activities don't need to be *just for toddlers or just for big kids or just for one kid at a time*. The right activity can achieve a balance and become a great equalizer for kids of all ages. It's like a toy that all the kids can play with together.

These activities are about creating a community feel and environment, like a watering hole in the savanna. It's a place for kids to come together and co-exist.

If I see kids are struggling to connect with each other, I often make an activity to get the ball rolling in the right direction. Don't underestimate just how powerful a communal activity can be as a tool to bring kids together.

WARNING

All activities need to be done under direct adult supervision. Use discretion for what is safe for your child and home. Reach out to your pediatrician if you have any questions about your child's safety with an activity.

GLOOP BAKING BIN

SUPPLIES

- Storage bin
- Cornstarch (also called maize starch or corn flour)
- Water
- Kitchen utensils
- Food coloring (optional)

HOW-TO

Let's talk about gloop. Gloop is an AMAZING part-liquid, part-solid, all-awesome substance. Here's how you make it: mix together two parts corn starch to one part water (for this giant bin, I used 4 cups of corn starch and 2 cups of water). Dye the water with a single drop of food coloring if you want. Stir to combine and pour the mixture into the bin. Add baking utensils.

WHY IT'S GOOD

Experimenting with gloop is science and sensory at its finest. The added baking supplies make for one amazing imaginary play setup.

WHAT ELSE

Gloop is taste-safe so it's a great sensory activity for even the youngest siblings. It's also fabulous in a dry bathtub and rinses down the drain easily with water added.

PAINT THE TOYS

SUPPLIES

- Plastic toys
- Washable paint
- Storage bin
- Ice cube tray

HOW-TO

Start by placing all the toys in the bin. Using a bin when painting is a great way to contain the mess, and so is putting the paint in ice cube trays as a make-shift palette.

When they're done, put the kids and the toys in the bathtub to clean everything off. Because the toys are plastic and the paint is washable, it comes right off in the tub and you get a two-for-one activity.

WHY IT'S GOOD

This is a "process art" activity for kids to freely create with. Kids have carte blanche to make decisions and express their own ideas. It's also a fine motor skills activity and a chance to practice pencil grip.

WHAT ELSE

You can make a theme for this activity and let your kids paint only one type of toy like trucks, dolls, or dinosaurs.

INDOOR BALL RAMP

SUPPLIES

- Large strip of cardboard
- All the balls
- Broomstick
- Painter's tape

HOW-TO

First, cut out a long strip of cardboard and curl the end. Next, tape a broomstick to the backside to make the ramp extra stable. Gather all the balls and let the rolling fun begin.

BONUS: Add a basket on the floor as a target.

WHY IT'S GOOD

This is a serious STEM activity with so much science and engineering happening. As children roll the balls down, they are learning about gravity, motion, and angles at an early childhood level.

WHAT ELSE

Keep this ramp up for a few days and let the kids move it around as needed. Encourage your kids to experiment with different objects, sizes, and shapes.

CREATION STATION

SUPPLIES

- Classy garbage (recycled materials)
- Glue
- Scissors

HOW-TO

Gather "classy garbage" from around your house and recycling bin, such as egg cartons, tissue paper, and ribbon. Store it all in a container or box. Invite your children to imagine and build anything they can think of. No rules or preset ideas—this is about your child using their imagination to freely create.

WHY IT'S GOOD

Tinkering is a powerful activity in early childhood. It promotes engineering, experimenting, imagination, and invention. When a child is tinkering, they are able to test their ideas and apply their curiosity.

WHAT ELSE

Consider keeping this box of classy garbage for a while—the more time a child has to invent, the more ambitious and experienced they become. The amount of time they spend tinkering will greatly improve their skills.

CARDBOARD ROAD

SUPPLIES

- Box
- Black permanent marker
- Various toys (animals, cars, and blocks)

HOW-TO

Find a large box and cut it open so it lies flat. On the box, draw a road map. Let your children create a city on the box.

WHY IT'S GOOD

There's a whole lot of imagination and creativity happening here, and also a lot of engineering at work.

WHAT ELSE

Plan to keep this box road out for a while. My kids keep it up for weeks at a time whenever we make one. It becomes a centerpiece of play in our house. Encourage kids to add to the city any toys they need.

COLOR MIXING STATION

SUPPLIES

- Medicine droppers, syringes, or turkey basters
- Small bowls or jars
- Water
- Food coloring (red, yellow, blue)
- Ice cube tray
- Storage bin

HOW-TO

Fill three small jars with dyed water: red, yellow, and blue (primary colors). Set an empty ice cube tray inside the empty bin to contain spills. Invite your kids to carefully mix the colored water into the ice cube slots. Show them how to use the syringes or droppers. Encourage them, initially, to mix only TWO colors in each slot. Dump the full tray into the bin and start over. Let them experiment by mixing with all three colors.

WHY IT'S GOOD

This activity is part science, part fine motor skills, and all magic and mystery to kids. Make sure to ask LOTS of questions before the activity begins. "What will happen when two colors mix?"

WHAT ELSE

When the activity is all done, encourage your children to turn this into a sort of "pouring station" similar to the one shown on page 135. This helps lengthen the amount of time kids will play with the activity.

MUD KITCHEN

SUPPLIES

- Storage bins
- Various kitchen utensils
- Water
- Mud
- Yard clippings

HOW-TO

In a three separate bins, provide mud, water, and yard clippings. Set out kitchen utensils and containers, and invite the kids to create mud kitchen specialties.

WHY IT'S GOOD

This activity is rooted in imaginative and dramatic play. Kids create concoctions, pretend food, and other imaginative things from their simple muddy supplies.

WHAT ELSE

Make this activity a routine—every time you prune bushes in the yard, set up this activity using the trimmings.

GIANT COLORING PAGE

SUPPLIES

- Box
- Black permanent marker
- Paint
- Tape

HOW-TO

Find a large box and cut it so that it will lie flat. Use a black permanent marker to draw a personalized coloring page on the flattened box. Have the kids suggest objects and draw them on the box as best you can. Hang the box on a fence, wall, or just set it on the ground. Have kids work together to paint their giant coloring page.

WHY IT'S GOOD

This larger-than-life activity is so inviting for a group of kids. It gives them a chance to paint and create together.

WHAT ELSE

Remember this activity at the holidays—it's super fun to make a giant seasonal themed piece of art with the kids. You can also leave this out for them to work on over a few days.

EXTREME BOXES

SUPPLIES

- Cardboard boxes
- Art supplies
- Cut-out paper shapes
- Stickers

HOW-TO

Grab large cardboard boxes for your kids to decorate but go extreme. First, tape up the flaps on the box to create some extra height. Give your children all the tools to decorate with: crayons, markets, dot markers, stickers, and cut-out paper shapes. DO NOT throw away these boxes. Instead, when done, put all the supplies back in the boxes and store them in the garage. When you need a quick activity, pull them out to continue the imagining and decorating.

WHY IT'S GOOD

This open-ended activity is rich with imagination. Each time your child adds to their box, they turn it into something new: a robot, a spaceship, a house, a car . . .

WHAT ELSE

Just another reminder to NOT throw away these boxes after the first day. Keep them going, with the art supplies stored safely inside the box, and invite the kids to keep decorating them. My longest box-streak was three months with the same set of boxes. If you have only one box, great! Have siblings work *together*.

BODY PAINT

SUPPLIES

- Oversized paper (this is kraft paper)
- Black permanent marker
- Paint

HOW-TO

On the floor, roll out a large section of paper. Have your child lie down on the paper and trace the outline of their body. Give them paint to fill in and decorate their paper body.

WHY IT'S GOOD

This is a process art activity because there is no expectation or plan for what the painting will look like when it's finished. It's also a chance for your child to show you how they see themselves.

WHAT ELSE

At the end, cut out the body art paintings and hang them up—even if it's just in the garage to startle Dad when he comes home from work.

24

THE 411 ON GETTING OUT OF THE HOUSE

Leaving the house with kids went from a giant undertaking to something I didn't think twice about. That can happen for you too.

As much as I love looking deeply into my toddler's eyes for hours on end, that just won't pass all the time in a day. And frankly, I'm going to lose my mind if we just keep staring at each other. I mean, he's a cute kid buuuut . . . this lady needs a change of scenery.

I know life with little kids can seem overwhelming.

I know it can feel like we are living each day by the seat of our pants.

I know the world seems scary, demanding, and judgmental.

We often have this idea that the best, easiest, and safest place for us to be with our kids is home. I get it! It's where we are successful and where we can best control the situations we face. We have all our tools at home. We have security at home.

On the other hand, when we are stuck living in an endless hamster wheel inside our house . . . well, that can be really hard too.

We have to leave our house with our kids. We can do this.

The world is out there waiting for your family. It has its low points (I know it's not all sunshine all the time—I get it), but by and large, it's a great world to be a part of.

I want nothing more than to empower you to see the opportunity you have to introduce your child to the world. To show them, help them, and teach them what it means to be a part of this world. It's time to learn how to venture out with your kids and make it as successful as possible.

Here's my question to you: If we never take our kids into public, how will they learn to be a member of society?

We have to teach them.

We have to guide them.

We have to model, model, model how to be part of our community.

That means we have to get up the gumption and teach ourselves how to leave the house with little kids. We can do this.

Three kids and grocery shopping . . . we learned and I was so proud. I still am.

The first step is to make it a habit: leave the house each day.

I know it's hard. I know it's a lot to pack up. I know it's a lot of variables and what-ifs, and what-nows, but friend, try to leave the house every single day.

Take this chance with your kids. I promise, it is rewarding and totally worth it.

We are social people. Our children are social beings. We are not meant to be cooped up in a house all day.

We all go stir-crazy. The kids get antsy. In my house, that's a recipe that ends with me snapping at the kids more than I'd like and the TV taking over a solid bulk of parenting.

That's not how I want things to be. That's not the parenting memory I want. So, I hit the reset button by consistently getting my kids out of the house.

Yes, we leave the house every day.

Well, almost every day. Obviously, we stay home plenty of days. Sick days happen. Stay-at-Home orders happen (sigh). There are days where they play insanely well and I'm not about to interrupt kids playing. This isn't about putting pressure on yourself to meet a goal you read in some parenting book or your kids won't go to college. This is about you learning that you can do this and how valuable it is *when you choose to do it, and to feel strong and empowered that you can.*

Let's be super clear: I'm not asking you to pack up the car tomorrow and take your kids to the zoo by yourself for the first time ever. Holy moly, that would be a lot to bite off all at once.

Once the "baby" was too big to be worn, this is how we rolled every Monday to get groceries.

Nothing like three kids in a public bathroom without a stroller. Now that's a skill.

Kate's first time sitting in a cart—she seems thrilled.

This is about teaching yourself what you can do with your kids—learning what's comfortable, finding out what's in your wheelhouse, and expanding your kids' world.

We are NOT talking about giant adventures (that's actually in chapter 25). We are talking about things like grocery shopping, wandering a store, or walking to a nearby park.

The goal is to get your children out of the house and feel safe and confident doing that.

We grow this skill *little by little*. I know you can do this. No matter what your family is like— you can learn to do this.

Leaving the house and venturing into public is a skill. Treat it as a valuable skill that you have the power to grow and develop—it's like learning to run a marathon. You have to train. As you get better at being in public, so will your kids. They will learn the social norms and routines of different places and stores. They will learn how to behave in various places or how rules vary (for example, my preschooler walks *next to the cart* at a grocery store but has to *sit in the cart* at a houseware store—too many tiny trinkets).

We can grow this skill. You are fully capable of doing this. Believe in yourself the same way that I believe in you and in your skills as a parent. This is doable. It is achievable.

MY TIPS FOR GETTING OUT OF THE HOUSE

Make a list of places where YOU currently shop. I'm going to assume you just wrote down Target and Costco. Don't decide to start getting out of the house by going somewhere you've never been. Keep this close to home and comfortable.

Parks and walks count! Don't think for a minute that walking to a local park doesn't count. It totally does. The point here is leaving the house, taking the kids in public, and breaking up the day.

Think about what you need to take with you for this trip. Do you really need four changes of clothes to go to the grocery store? Overpacking is often our downfall. When we overpack, we overthink, we can't find what we actually need, and we can accidentally cause even more stress. Bring only what you most critically need, and store some backups in the car.

The drive-thru works too! Sometimes when my kids are sick or I just don't want to unload and reload and unload and reload them, we head for the drive-thru. They're buckled and contained, it's 20 minutes to drive there and back, we listen to the radio, I get a coffee, and we've all taken a break. Sometimes, I've been known to drive one town over to a different drive-thru in the name of a longer car ride break.

Ask for help. The world is ready to help you. You just need to look up and confidently ask for it. "Could you grab that for me?" "Will you hold this?" "I need help getting my kids and this to my car. Any chance you'd help another parent out?" It is a BEAUTIFUL teachable moment to show your children it's OK to ask for help and how lovely is it to help another. This is HUGE.

We want to raise responsible children who look for chances to help. We also want children to willingly ask for help instead of struggling in silence. When we lead and show by example (model, model, model!), we leave a powerful lesson in our children's hearts. Don't get discouraged by needing help. Rejoice in the chance to show your kids how awesome it is to ask and give help.

WHAT ARE THE BENEFITS OF GETTING OUT?

It's a big world out there and our children will need to live in it someday. They learn to live in it by watching us.

When we order everything online or always have our groceries delivered or head to the pickup line at box stores, we are making OUR lives more convenient.

But we aren't making our kids' FUTURES more convenient.

I'm never trying to make you feel guilty. Trust me, my mail carrier knows me by name and I should have bought stock in online companies years ago. But when I have the chance, I choose to take the kids on an errand with me because they need to see that.

I often think: "OK, yeah . . . I can order this online, BUT we don't have anything going on tomorrow and we can run into town quickly to grab it."

I choose to inconvenience my own life a little bit because these moments provide a lot of learning opportunities for our kids.

When we are out in public with our kids, never forget that they're doing some serious learning at the same time.

Things kids are learning when out:

One of the first times Sam (4) and Kate (2.5) got to order and pay on their own.

- **Socializing:** They are learning to talk to strangers (the good kind of strangers) and seeing a variety of people, not just their family. Socializing doesn't only happen in day cares and preschools—it happens in the world all around us.

- **Self-control:** As much as we want to buy everything we see and like, we can't. Having that open conversation with your kids (and modeling it with your own wants and needs) is a huge discussion in stores. This dialogue gets missed with online shopping.

- **Money management:** Seeing an exchange of money for merchandise is something kids don't see often enough anymore. Talking about what a credit card is really helps and letting them be part of the paying process does too. Paying in cash is the most awesome example if you have it on you.

- **Basic life rules:** We can model for kids how all humans follow basic rules— we don't run in stores, we use soft voices, we don't push in line. These are all expectations we have for our children, but if we aren't going into stores with them to model it . . . how will they master these basic boundaries in their own lives? Especially consider the connection between store behavior and school behavior—these experiences help. Children often assume rules are a kid-only part of life. It's important they learn that rules are a part of everyone's lives.

- **Conversation and language development:** Lots of new terms, phrases, and vocabulary words can be learned outside the home. Think of all the things a department store has that your home does not. This is a great chance for conversation—to talk and discuss, make guesses about products, and work on growing language skills.

- **Handling boredom:** All of life is not wild and crazy and exciting. There are times when it is dull. These are learning moments for our kids as they grow in their ability to self-entertain. Kids need "under-stimulating" moments to figure out their own ways to keep their minds occupied.

- **Expanding their background knowledge:** Life experience is a big deal in the early years of schooling. How much background knowledge a child has can help them better comprehend stories they read and apply mathematical principles more easily. Without life experiences away from the home, children have a harder time making connections to their learning and the information being presented at school.

A FEW QUICK NOTES ABOUT LITTLE KIDS AND STORES

No one wants to leave a store with a screaming child.

No one wants to deal with an "I want this!" standoff.

Going to stores full of fun things that kids want to buy can seem very, very daunting. The truth is? They just need to get desensitized, used to it, and all trained up on the process.

1. **Kids are fast learners.**
   As long as you establish you aren't going to leave with a toy or prize, kids learn quickly what the status quo is. Make sure to talk about this. Set the expectation and give information before you walk into the store. "Today is not a toy buying day, but we can go look at toys, get ideas, and build our wish lists!"

2. **Try to go to the same stores.**
   Getting to know the checkers at our local grocery store is the best thing I ever did. For my kids, going to the same store is part of their routine and takes away any unknowns that come with an unfamiliar store. My kids love to guess which checkers will be there to say "Hi!" to them, and they look for specific workers throughout the store. (I've also made a point to say hi and chat with the checkers over the years—this helped build our relationship too.)

3. **Be OK with saying NO.**

   Stores are a great place to set up boundaries and model the concept of needs versus wants. Talk openly with your child about what you're buying versus what you're not buying. Say things like "Wow, I really want this candle, but I don't need it." Model the needs versus wants dilemma. Show them that even you don't get to buy everything you want.

A loading up selfie—leaving the house for who knows where.

BUT WHAT ABOUT SCREENS?

Screens are a tool (see page 276 for my tips on screens), but if we use a device for every trip to the hardware store, we miss out on so many teachable moments.

Limit screens when you're out of the home so your kids aren't reliant on them. Even more, do it for your future self when you really need the screen to buy some time and it's a magical tool they're excited to have.

When my husband and I were picking out kitchen cabinets at the most boring showroom in the world, our kids (then ages 5, 3, and 18-months-old) were so excited to share a single iPad.

Just a mom . . . in her car . . . heading to a drive-thru . . . for sanity . . .

WHAT HAPPENS IF THE OUTING IS A DISASTER?

Leave. Abandon ship. Turn around. *But keep your head held high.*

We all have times when everything goes bonkers. What separates us is our willingness to try again. Learn from what happened and try again, I beg of you. You won't be the only parent that day to leave the store unexpectedly. These things just happen. Don't feel defeated by them. Instead, learn from it. Be impressed by your willingness to walk away and then, even more impressed by your willingness to try again.

I PROMISE, YOU CAN DO THIS AND IT'S WORTH IT.

You can learn to leave the house and you can be successful at it. It's the type of skill that comes little by little, by building up your courage. As you become more comfortable, your kids become more comfortable—and the experience and ease exponentially grows.

You'll never feel prouder than the day you conquer a big box store alone with kids. Trust me, that is a magical moment of pride you don't want to miss.

TAKEAWAY MESSAGE

I'll say it again for the back of the class: you can do this. Leaving the house with kids doesn't have to be an impossible mountain to summit that's only doable with another adult next to you. You are enough for your children. We often build things up as way more complicated and challenging than they really are. As parents, our job is to guide our kids and show them how to live in the world beyond us . . . this is how we start practicing for that inevitable day.

MY DIAPER BAG - A TALE OF THEN AND NOW

FIRST BABY	THIRD BABY
• 6–8 diapers	• 1 diaper
• Full pack of wipes	• A few wipes thrown in a baggie
• Portable changing pad	• 1 onesie (two sizes too small)
• Baby booger wipes	• (Everything shoved in a purse, not a diaper bag)
• 3–4 loud toys	
• Several snack options	
• Muslin blanket	
• Hand sanitizer	
• Sanitizing wipe	
• Diaper cream	
• Multiple pacifiers in different styles	
• Teething rings	
• 1 bib	
• Scented diaper trash bags	
• Kid silverware	
• Nursing cover	
• 3 onesies	
• 1 pair of pants	
• Several pairs of socks	
• Baby nail trimmers	
• Baby hair brush	
• Top for parent in case of spit-up	

25

GO BIG OR GO HOME - IT'S ADVENTURE DAY!

Going on small errands was the first hill to climb . . . then I was ready for mountain-sized adventures with my kids.

Simple errands and going to the grocery store are great reasons to leave the house every day. As I grew in my ability to take my kids out in public alone, I started to get the itch: I wanted more. I wanted adventures with them.

In my parenting journey, I realized I could make a big impact on our week by adding one big adventure day.

Adventure days are more than errands. More than going to the park across the street. More than running over to your bestie's house.

Wait.

Pause.

Hear me LOUD AND CLEAR.

Rome and adventure days were not built in, well, a day. I didn't wake up one morning and decide, "I can totally take three kids to the museum. This will be no problem."

I built us up to big adventures by getting comfortable taking my kids on smaller ones. For a long time in my life, going to the store was our adventure day and I was so proud of myself for getting us there. I still am.

But as I became more comfortable with my children and their behaviors in public (I knew what to expect, what their triggers were, what to avoid), I started taking steps toward larger adventures—going to the zoo, driving to a beach, heading to a play space.

I made a list of places to take the kids where I felt comfortable, where I felt safe, and where I knew my way around. Everyone's comfort level is different because all parents are different. Even my husband and I (with the same three kids!) have different places we feel comfortable taking the kids on our own.

I choose to do these big adventures to give my kids the life experiences they need and to also fill my memory bank full of happy days to look back on when they're older. This isn't just about the kids, you know.

Remember, start small. Let yourself get comfortable. Trust that you can guide and monitor your kids safely. Find places where you feel good. Ask for help when you need it. And look for others who might need help too.

You can do this. Little by little you can. I believe in you and in your parenting.

ADVENTURE DAY TIP: MEMBERSHIPS AND PUNCH CARDS

Adventure days don't have to cost an arm and a leg, and one of the most cost-effective ways to have adventures is to ask for memberships and punch cards as gifts. Have a kid's birthday coming up? Ask Grandma for a zoo membership. Tell your uncle that your kiddo loves the local play area. Having these cards and memberships is a huge blessing and a way to make memories without breaking any banks. Just be willing to ask for them as gifts.

All loaded up with three kids in the car—that was a workout. Oh em gee.

MY FIRST ADVENTURE DAY WITH THREE KIDS

My third-born child was five weeks old when I decided to go on our first adventure day alone as a mom with three kids. I would say I was "proficient" at adventure day outings when I had two kids, so adding a third—although difficult—wasn't totally out of my wheelhouse. I chose a small family-friendly mall near our home for my very first adventure with three kids.

I thought I had timed it just right so the baby would be falling asleep when we got there. But of course not. He napped the whole way there, and by the time we unloaded and got inside the mall, he was screaming, hungry, and I had no idea how to sit and feed him with two toddlers. I may have been slightly in over my head, but we were already there so I decided to press on with our adventure.

I found a bench near a quarter-operated kiddie ride. I thought I could keep my two toddlers on that while feeding the baby. As I tried to help my 21-month-old onto the ride while juggling a screaming newborn and answering the 57 questions from my three-year-old, I heard a woman shouting, "WAIT!!! WAIT!! I'm coming to help!"

She had a toddler, a preschooler, a bag of quarters, and I'm fairly certain she also had angel wings, but I can't totally remember.

As she loaded the quarter machine for my kids, she sat across from me and said, "I've been there. I have three kids too, and someone helped me once like this. I've been waiting two years to pay it forward."

She added a few more quarters to the ride, fed my kids a snack from her bag, and helped us load back up for the rest of our adventure—which ended up going great after that one opening hiccup.

That moment taught me so much about parenting and helping others and not being afraid to ask for help or offer help. We are one big parenting team and life is so much sweeter when we remember we are in this together.

MY QUICK TIP TO HELP YOU START ADVENTURE DAYS

Start your adventure days with a friend.

See? I told you it was a quick tip.

If the idea of taking your kids out on big adventures—like the children's museum, a new park, the beach—overwhelms you, please remember a few things:

- We all feel overwhelmed in the beginning.
- Your friend might be feeling the same thing.

Find a friend and form an adventure day posse. Work together to take the kids out. You won't believe how simple and efficient adventure days can be until you try them with another parent. Double the parents means double the hands, double the eyes, and double the confidence.

It's a powerful thing to combine forces with another parent and recognize there is strength in numbers. You can do so much more if you are willing to invite a friend to try with you.

Take seven kids and one newborn to a creek? This could only happen for us as a team.

Or maybe you have a friend who you know is already really good at adventure days. Ask if you can tag along. If you want this for your children and you want adventure days for yourself, be willing to say, "Hey, you're really good at this. Can we come with you so I can learn how?"

Conquering a place that is initially scary and overwhelming with the safety net of a friend will help you map out how to do it on your own.

Suddenly, the aquarium doesn't seem so daunting. You've seen how it works. You've got a game plan. You've been successful here before.

Make yourself an adventure day posse. Reach out to others and parent together. We are so strong when we work together, and it's an important way to build community for our children. Seek out others to play with because a strong posse can help you soar.

HOW TO END ADVENTURES WITHOUT A MELTDOWN

There is nothing worse than having a great adventure day spoiled by an epic meltdown at the end. It taints the whole memory.

We know exactly what it looks like. We plan and execute a fabulous day filled with memories for our kids. It's late in the morning or day, and suddenly the crying begins. They're tired. They're hungry. They're mad at a kid who looked at them the wrong way. Before we know it, it's not only time to leave, but we literally have to leave RIGHT NOW. It's an ASAP situation.

My mom had a tip that I remember her using when I was child. She reminded me to use it when I was a nanny in high school, again when I was a teacher, and by the time I had my own kids, her little trick was just a part of my normal routine.

Leave before the meltdown starts.

We all know about how long our kids can last on an outing. That's part of the experience that small errands and leaving the house teaches us. We know roughly how much time something will be successful before our kids fall apart from exhaustion, hunger, overstimulation, or all of the above.

Learn this.

For my kids, they can go about 60 minutes at a play area before they start swarming for a snack and I can usually get about 30 minutes more. At 90 minutes, I know it's better to call it early and end the play on my terms, rather than risk the Meltdown Chorus beginning to sing.

Routines provide another cue that lets me know I need to leave. If we aren't having lunch at the place, we need to leave an activity by 12:00 p.m. to be home in time for lunch and naps. I know our routine and I know my kids' habits, and I do everything I can to set them up for success.

This was their "one last thing to do" moment— running up a grassy hill before heading home.

Even if my kids are still having fun and feeling happy and excited, I know the meltdown and tears are right around the corner. It's better to get out before the drama than try to squeeze in a few more minutes.

Once the meltdown has started, it's always too late. Stay ahead of the curve. Be proactive. The goal is to leave on a high note and make happiness the last memory of the adventure.

When I'm ready for us to leave, I give the kids a solid warning. Even though time is abstract for kids, I say something like, "We are getting close to the end and will be leaving soon." I never spring it on my kids that we are leaving and immediately need to go. That's not fair to them and their play. They need time to tie up loose ends.

Once it's actually time to go, I take a page from our favorite animated TV tiger and tell my kids we are now in the "leaving process" and they need to pick one last thing to do. This gives them autonomy and ownership of leaving. They get to make a final decision. Once they're done with that last thing, they know it's time to go home.

This process works.

Being proactive works. So much of parenting has to do with anticipating their needs and potential pitfalls. This is just another chance to practice that skill.

The more you do this, the more routine it becomes. My kids understand the expectation and the system, and they aren't surprised or upset by leaving. They know the drill.

Leaving on a high note is so important. Adventures are that much sweeter if our last memory is a happy one. Getting in the habit of leaving before the tears makes adventures that much more enjoyable and makes it more likely you will plan another one.

WHAT IF THE KIDS DON'T WANT TO LEAVE?

What if we tell the kids it's time to pick one last thing before heading home, but that starts a meltdown? "I don't want to leave! I'm having fun!"

Here's how to handle it: get down on their level, look them in the eyes, and say, "I am so happy you had so much fun! Let's make a plan to come back soon. Right now, it is time to leave. Don't miss your chance to pick one last thing to do." Stay firm and remain clear and consistent with the expectations and the plan. We always use the same exit procedure for that very reason.

26

ASK FOR A PROOF OF MOM PHOTO

Before I started taking "proof of mom" photos, finding pictures of me with my kids was impossible. They just didn't exist.

A while back, I did an interview for a website and they asked for the unthinkable—a photo of me with my kids. I know! How dare they ask me for a picture where I'm actually with all my children.

I frantically dug around and came up with a few GREAT options (nope, this is just sarcasm). My options were: a terribly lit, shaky selfie OR quickly take a new photo that morning and hope for the best and that's what we did. That's the photo you're looking at now.

When I said I had a few options, I actually meant I had two options. Literally two options and one of them didn't even technically exist yet.

I'm a natural picture taker. I've always over-documented my life, from high school and beyond. Having an iPhone just made things even easier. Now I could over-document without anyone batting an eye. They expected it. And to top that off, I'm an Instagrammer, so taking photos is what I do.

But somehow in all the over-documenting of my family's lives, I forgot to document my own. I forgot that my life matters too, and having myself in photos is important too.

I forgot that my kids need to see I was there (not just hear me telling them, "Oh, well, I was the one who took those photos.")

I forgot that I need to see a record of myself growing up in motherhood and life.

I deserve to be remembered in pictures, too.

As I stared at my computer that day, letting the full weight of my photo-less existence wash over me, I will tell you this: I didn't blame anyone else for it.

This wasn't my husband's fault for forgetting to take pictures of me. (Really, it definitely was not his fault. He didn't even have a smartphone yet. He finally does now . . . barely.)

This was my fault.

I didn't ask. I didn't think about it.

I didn't put two and two together or think about how it would feel to look back at early motherhood and have only a handful of photos. And an even smaller handful of photos with me and ALL my kids. And an even smaller, smaller handful that weren't selfies.

It had to change.

I'm busting my buns over here to make memories, go on these adventures, and make our day-to-day life run smoothly, but you know what? I want to be remembered in those memories too.

I don't think it's selfish to say, "I want there to be a record of me with my family."

In fact, I think it's the opposite. I want my kids to have these pictures and to love them long after I'm gone. "There she is! Look at Mom!"

One of my favorite "proof of mom" photos—everyone is almost smiling so that's a win.

I identified my goal: get in the photo.

But this wouldn't be the type of goal where I could say it into the wind and hope for change, like most every other goal I make. This one would become a cornerstone mission in my life.

It's been years since I made this goal and now I call them "proof of mom" photos. I take them on every major adventure with my kids.

It's proof I was there, behind the scenes, making everything work like clockwork—and I was having an awesome time. It's proof of my existence on all those fun days together.

When we go to the zoo or have a beach day or take a fun hike, I stop for a second and take a proof of mom photo. Something about having that catch phrase ("proof of mom!") helped me remember to take them.

One little hiccup on this quest for photos with all my kids is that I'm out alone with them 90% of the time, so if I want proof of mom photos, I have to ask for help.

Gasp. Yes, that means talking to strangers!

I know this is hard.

Do it for the greater good. Do it for your future self and your future kids.

I usually ask another parent with kids. I say it just like this, "Hi! Can you take a proof of mom photo for me so I can actually be in a picture and get a little credit for all that I'm doing with them?"

They laugh and say yes every. single. time. No one has ever turned me down.

No shower that day, no make-up yet. I love this one. I'm so glad I asked for it to be taken.

In fact, half the time they ask for a proof of mom or dad photo too. And that's the way it should be. We should be helping each other be in those photos.

When I'm old and gray (which feels right around the corner . . .), these photos will mean everything to me, and I hope they'll mean as much to my kids. No one will care if I showered or was perfectly dressed, if my makeup was just right, or if this kid or that one was in a bad mood. I know that 36-year-old Susie will look pretty awesome to those 80-year-old eyes no matter what.

TAKEAWAY MESSAGE

Ask for the photos. Get in the photos. Be proud of yourself and your efforts. These years go by fast and as cliche as it is, the memories and the pictures really are all we will have left. Make sure there is proof of mom (or dad, parent, caregiver, etc.).

27

ACTIVITIES FOR OUTINGS

Keeping a toddler occupied on an airplane means bringing all the activities.

Activities don't have to be an at-home-only thing.

I bring activities with me as a proactive tool to use if my kids will be asked to sit, stay, and be on the quieter side of life for more than a few minutes. This helps keep the kids busy and keeps them off my cell phone. It's a real win-win.

When kids are being asked to sit still and comply in public, that's a tall order. We can help them learn these skills of self-entertainment by bringing a few tools from home (remember, adults flip through magazines, read books, and play on their phones during wait times—our kids deserve something to do too).

Being a proactive parent means seeing the fire before it starts, and you can see a fire brewing when you lock siblings in a doctor's office waiting for a checkup.

Be proactive. Think through the situation. Bring a few items or have some simple setups on hand to quickly make a giant difference in your child's life and behavior.

WARNING

All activities need to be done under direct adult supervision. Use discretion for what is safe for your child and home. Reach out to your pediatrician if you have any questions about your child's safety with an activity.

THE RESTAURANT KIT AND HOW IT CHANGES EVERYTHING

This is a restaurant kit. It's also my travel kit, doctor's office kit, and going-somewhere-boring kit for my kids. Since 2016, this restaurant kit has saved my life whenever we go somewhere my kids need to wait or sit quietly.

The name of the game is meltdown prevention and being one step ahead. Having a small kit like this goes a long way. I keep mine in my car so it's always with me. I don't want to be caught in an emergency quiet time situation without it. I have one kit for all three kids to share, so the items inside span a wide age range.

Here's what's in my kit:

- Deck of cards
- Box of crayons
- Three toy cars
- A few plastic animals
- Index cards
- Dot stickers
- Regular stickers
- Sticky notes
- A black marker (for me to use)

I place all these items in a wipes container and it is PLENTY to occupy my kids and keep them busy enough to stay out of trouble. It's nothing fancy, but it is truly life-changing.

DOCTOR'S OFFICE
DOT STICKERS

SUPPLIES

- Dot stickers
- Washable marker

HOW-TO

In the doctor's office, draw lines, names, shapes, or anything on the paper covering the table. Hand your kids dot stickers and let them cover the lines.

WHY IT'S GOOD

The doctor's office is a hard room to be in and this provides a little fun. It's an activity that takes a lot of concentration and fine motor skills.

WHAT ELSE

Don't forget to remove the white sticky part of the sheet (the part that surrounds the dots) to make it easier for little hands to grasp.

TRAVEL SNACKS

SUPPLIES

- Colorful circular cereal
- String
- Tape

HOW-TO

While waiting in the airport or on a long road trip, let your child build their own travel snack. First, cut the string to length and wrap a piece of tape around ONE end. This makes a kind of needle. On the opposite end, tie a knot around one piece of cereal to create a stopping point that locks all the other cereal pieces in place. Let your child thread the necklace. Once the necklace is done, tie it and let your child wear it as a snack to eat on the plane or in the car.

WHY IT'S GOOD

This gives kids a project and something to do in a tough, boring situation. It also gives them a go-to snack they can eat independently during travel.

WHAT ELSE

Worried about airport germs? I get it. Wipe off the seat your child is working on first and consider placing a towel or sweatshirt under them.

DOCTOR'S OFFICE ROAD

SUPPLIES

- Washable marker
- Toy cars

HOW-TO

On the paper lining the doctor's office bed, draw a road for your kids to play with. Hand them cars and trucks to play with as they pass the time waiting for the doctor.

WHY IT'S GOOD

It's an imaginary play setup that draws their attention away from the sometimes scary doctor visit situation.

WHAT ELSE

This is also a great activity for paper tablecloths at restaurants or to carry with you on construction paper. Create a small road on paper, slip it into your bag, and pull it out for an instant activity while kids are waiting (see a photo of this on page 224, where my youngest is playing while the airplane is boarding).

MINI-STICKER LINEUP

SUPPLIES

- Index cards
- Marker
- Small stickers

HOW-TO

On the index cards, draw various lines and shapes (even your child's name). Give your child the small stickers to decorate and line up across the index cards.

WHY IT'S GOOD

This is a fine motor skill workout. It is meticulous and takes time, quiet, and patience to build the lineups.

WHAT ELSE

Pack this activity in a reusable zipper pouch that lives in your car or bag. It's a great mess-free, low-prep activity to pull out when you need instant help.

WHAT'S MISSING

SUPPLIES

- Anything you have with you (literally anything)

HOW-TO

This simple memory game is easy to play wherever you are and with whatever you have. Use things from the diaper bag, your car, backpack, or a table at a restaurant. Select four items. Repeat the names of the items in order and out loud. Have your child close their eyes. Remove or cover one item and ask your child, "What's missing?"

WHY IT'S GOOD

Talk about an amazing activity for vocabulary and communication skills! This activity is also great for introducing game play to young toddlers and is still fun to play with elementary-aged children.

WHAT ELSE

Teach your child how to hide objects from you. Practice taking turns hiding and guessing. Model sportsmanship and good game-playing skills.

28

STOP WORRYING ABOUT YOUR TODDLER AND ACADEMICS

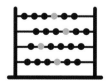

Teaching was my dream job and I loved it. I walked down the road of learning with hundreds of five-, six-, and seven-year-olds, and it was a joy. I may have left the classroom when I had my first baby, but my heart stayed in school . . . which is why I'm increasingly concerned about what's happening today with kids and education.

"My toddler isn't learning enough."

"They're already three. Shouldn't they know that?"

"I'm worried my four-year-old is behind in reading."

Nothing breaks my heart more than the academic pressures being placed on young children today.

In the past two decades, there's been a massive shift toward academics in early childhood.[1] There's so much beautiful learning happening in these early years but in the attempt to *make children smarter*, our focus has been pulled away from deep learning and placed onto simple, basic skills—skills that can be tested. Our kids deserve more.

Now, before you close this book because I'm saying EXACTLY the opposite of everything you're hearing from friends and family and seeing on social media . . . hear me out for a few more sentences.

We want the sun and the moon for our kids. We want to do everything possible to make sure they have happy lives. We are working so hard in early childhood to set them up for a lifetime of success. There are skills and learning that need to happen in the early years, but sadly, they are not what's valued today. (I promise I'll get to what skills and learning we *should* value. It's coming.)

Today, the goal is academics.

1 Carlsson-Paige N, McLaughlin GB, Almon JW. Reading Instruction in Kindergarten: Little Gain and Much to Lose. Defending the Early Years; Alliance for Childhood; 2014. https://deyproject.files.wordpress.com/2015/01/readinginkindergarten_online-1.pdf.

The goal is to pump information into young children and essentially fill them up with as much knowledge as possible to get them started "right" in life. Parents have been fed the idea that things like remembering the ABCs and counting the 123s are massive developmental milestones in early childhood that kids need to reach as soon as possible. We're told if kids aren't mastering or immersed in these academics from the get-go, their futures hang in the balance. This isn't true.[2]

There's so much more to early childhood than academics. It's more than flash cards, tablet apps, and computer-based learning. It's way more than learning the alphabet and counting. Our kids have important learning to do, learning that will influence and affect their whole lives—really complex learning that will help them through school and life beyond.

Here's a fun tip: learning the ABCs and the 123s isn't as complex a skill as you might think . . .

> **Learning the ABCs and 123s is just memorizing. It's no different than memorizing colors, shapes, construction vehicles, animal names, princesses, or dinosaur types, but for some reason we have put these two particular memorized skills on pedestals and we use them as the measurement tools to judge all early childhood learning against.**

This has got to stop.

The idea that how quickly a child can remember the name of a symbol (like a letter) or the sequence of words in a phrase (which is all rote counting is) will somehow dictate their future success is outrageous.

These skills are just memorizing and in the grand scheme of learning, memorizing is a low-level, basic skill.[3] Our society has, unfortunately, chosen the lowest form of learning as the benchmark standard to judge childhood against. While our kids will need the ABCs

---

2   Marcon RA. Moving up the grades: relationship between preschool model and later school success. Early Childhood Research and Practice. 2002;4(1). https://www.researchgate.net/publication/26390914_Moving_up_the_Grades_Relationship_between_Preschool_Model_and_Later_School_Success.

3   Armstrong P. Bloom's Taxonomy. Vanderbilt University. https://cft.vanderbilt.edu/guides-sub-pages/blooms-taxonomy/.

and 123s *someday* in their education, this isn't the kind of skill to use as a measurement tool for success or to worry incessantly over in the early years.

On top of the obsession with teaching children low-level memorizing skills is the equally concerning obsession with teaching them these skills as early as possible. Instead of valuing the natural pace a child learns and honoring their body's development, pressure is placed on parents and children to learn quickly.

In previous generations, children went to kindergarten *to learn the ABCs*. Now when a three-year-old doesn't know them, many families are worried, wracked with guilt, and harbor feelings of failure and disappointment. This isn't the way it used to be. This isn't the way it's supposed to be.

It's important to note that children learn the ABCs anytime from age two until sometime in kindergarten,[4] which has been documented for decades. Think of how big that age range is! This isn't a small developmental window like when they're learning to roll over or sit up, which most kids meet within a matter of weeks or months from one to the next. This is a giant canyon of time with years separating one child from the next.

Your child will fall somewhere in that range. Kids develop at different rates—you know that! Learning letters and numbers is simply a skill that our kids will learn when they are developmentally ready.

Think of it like this—you wouldn't force a 6-month-old to walk or make an 18-month-old ride a two-wheeled pedal bike. We wouldn't do that! We know better! We know that developmentally, a 6-month-old isn't ready to walk, and an 18-month-old needs a lot of other motor skills and maturity before they're ready to pedal a two-wheeled bike. We respect the child's growth and development.

Treat academics in early childhood the same way.

Most parents already value and acknowledge natural motor skill development in children—we understand it intrinsically and deeply. We can see how these skills unfold

4 National Research Council. Preventing Reading Difficulties in Young Children. Washington, DC: The National Academies Press; 1998. DOI: 10.17226/6023. https://files.eric.ed.gov/fulltext/ED416465.pdf.

and grow in their own time. We need to remember that learning academic skills is no different from learning motor skills. And we need to start valuing them and honoring them in the same way—without rushing their development.

It is well documented that children have followed the same basic path of milestones and development for the last 100 years,[5] but only in recent years have we changed our expectations and attempted to hurry children's academic growth.[6]

Let your child develop on their own schedule . . . not someone else's. Honor the person your child is.

We know that a child who started walking at 10 months old won't be better at walking later in life than a child who started walking at 15 months old. Learning the ABCs early is not an indication of future academic success—whenever your child memorizes them won't define them.

Unless there are underlying conditions or learning disabilities present, it doesn't matter how early or "late" kids learn the ABCs. Your toddler might memorize construction trucks. They might memorize princesses. They might memorize the ABCs. Be OK with where your child is on their developmental path because there is so much more to your child and their early childhood education than these basic skills.

Early childhood life shouldn't be about forcing kids into academics. Academics will happen, but remember your child needs a solid foundation of knowledge and understanding before these skills make sense. We can't teach a child the letter F is for flower and have it mean something until they know what a flower is and have interacted with it.

Early childhood is the time for complex learning that is beyond basic memorized academics . . . They need real skills and real learning that will someday support their growth and success in school.

5 Guddemi, Sambrook A, Wells S, et al. Arnold Gesell's developmental assessment revalidation substantiates child-oriented curriculum. SAGE Open. 2014;4(2). DOI: 10.1177/2158244014528918. https://cdn.shopify.com/s/files/1/2084/3047/files/Published_GDO_Study.pdf?2297550519868886760.

6 Carlsson-Paige N, McLaughlin GB, Almon JW. Reading Instruction in Kindergarten: Little Gain and Much to Lose. Defending the Early Years; Alliance for Childhood; 2014. https://deyproject.files.wordpress.com/2015/01/readinginkindergarten_online-1.pdf.

WHAT ARE THE SKILLS TO FOCUS ON?

For generations before today, the early childhood years were a time for developing social skills, exploration, playtime and imagination, hands-on learning, discovery, art, and creativity. It used to be a time when we valued the less visible or "soft" skills—the immeasurable life skills that need to be learned and have their foundations formed in the early years.[7]

That's what it was like for our generation. Think back to our early childhood years: We played. We made art. We created. We ran outside and we learned a lot of foundational skills for life. We went to kindergarten not knowing the alphabet and we learned to read in first and second grade. Our children are not leading the same lives.

Now we've been told to shift our focus to academics for our young children, and if a skill isn't measurable on a standardized test, it's not important. Gone are the days of unbridled exploration and play in the early years . . . they've been replaced by flash cards, worksheets, desks, and testing.[8]

We need to change this.

The OVER-valuation of academics in early childhood is causing us to UNDER-value, UNDER-teach, and UNDER-appreciate the real, actual, important skills kids need to learn in these years. I'm not trying to tease or clickbait it—don't worry, I'll explain the "real skills" shortly.

Today, we hold up a child's skills in the ABCs and 123s as the sole measure of their future success and that's just not right.

So, what's the real indicator of future success in a child?
The development of social and emotional skills in early childhood.

---

7 Shala M. The impact of preschool social-emotional development on academic success of elementary school students. Psychology. 2013;4(11):787–791. DOI: 10.4236/psych.2013.411112. https://www.scirp.org/html/39511. html.

8 Carlsson-Paige N, McLaughlin GB, Almon JW. Reading Instruction in Kindergarten: Little Gain and Much to Lose. Defending the Early Years; Alliance for Childhood; 2014. https://deyproject.files.wordpress.com/2015/01/readinginkindergarten_online-1.pdf.

Research shows time and time again that how well a child has developed these so-called soft skills plays a key role in how successful a child will be in their future schooling and beyond in adulthood.[9]

We need to worry about the whole child, not the academic child.

Rather than worrying about your toddler memorizing a few letters or some numbers, let's focus on developing skills that will carry them through life and learning.

Turn your focus to the social and emotional skills.

Make sure those are the skills being learned in early childhood because they are the most important. From their personal lives to social skills to academics, these soft skills are what we should hold on a pedestal in early childhood.

That's what every generation before us did.

WHAT ARE THESE 'SOFT' SOCIAL-EMOTIONAL SKILLS?

- **Taking risks**
- **Empathizing**
- **Questioning**
- **Relationships with others**
- **Problem-solving**
- **Being intrinsically motivated**
- **Having curiosity**
- **High self-esteem**
- **Communicating**
- **Self-regulating**
- **Exhibiting self-control**

9 Jones DE, Greenberg M, Crowley M. Early social-emotional functioning and public health: the relationship between kindergarten social competence and future wellness. American Journal of Public Health. 2015;105:2283–2290. DOI: 10.2105/AJPH.2015.302630. https://ajph.aphapublications.org/doi/10.2105/AJPH.2015.302630.

Living and parenting in an era where tangible skills are much more valued than intangible skills, I understand how the ABCs and 123s (or any other basic academic skill) became the benchmark value of a child. It's more fun to show off a toddler reciting the alphabet than a toddler who has exceptional self-regulating skills. Counting to 100 seems cooler to other parents than having great risk management skills.

But these soft skills are the ones to know. They are the be-all and end-all of early childhood. This is the learning our kids need to be doing (Want to know the best way to develop them in your child? The answer is in Chapter 30).

Think of your future child and their needs.

Consider your child in high school. Academics have gotten tougher and more high-level. They're challenging. What drives learning at that age is a child's intrinsic motivation to know more, their self-esteem to believe they can, and their ability to problem-solve. Questioning skills and communication skills also come into play as older children work through different subject matter. Without these soft skills, academics in high school will be a mountain for them—it won't matter how early they learned the ABCs if they have no self-motivation to keep climbing.

Think of peer pressure on teenagers and how crucial it is that they have high self-esteem, resilience, and risk management skills. Think of how important it is for older children to understand that failure happens. What happens to the child without reasoning skills when faced with a difficult dilemma? What happens to the teen without self-control?

The challenge for parents is making a giant mental shift away from OVER-valuing the basic, low-level memorization skills and instead celebrate our children learning incredibly high-level thinking skills—the same skills our parents valued in us during our childhood.

Focus on the skills your child does have (the really important ones) and the things your child loves. Look at all the ways they are learning and growing—in more complex ways than memorizing.

We can be the parents who go back to valuing real skills in early childhood. We can go back to valuing the whole child, not just the academic child.

EXPOSURE AND EXPERIENCE

Early childhood learning boils down to the "two Es"—exposure and experience. Kids need exposure and experience to help facilitate their academic learning in the future. Academic learning relies heavily on background knowledge. Focus on giving your child a breadth of exposures and experiences in these early years that they can draw on for their future learning. Think of all the previous knowledge kids pull from when learning about properties of liquids (remember that pouring station on page 135). Imagine trying to learn about engineering without a history of block building. These little moments children have working and interacting with their environment might seem small now, but those exposures and experiences will add up as they head into the school years.

Just so we are clear—here is a non-stressful way to introduce the ABCs:

Step 1: Throw away the flash cards.

Step 2: Take a deep breath.

You know your child will pick up the alphabet (and numbers!) at their own pace and there are more important skills to focus on in early childhood. But maybe you are still wondering . . . how will learning the ABCs develop naturally?

Here's how: Learning the alphabet develops in context, the same way memorizing animal names and their sounds develops in context. It's exactly the same—first you name an object and then you give the sound it makes. See how similar it is?

When you think about a child learning animal names and sounds, no one stresses over that skill. No one hovers over the child and searches the Internet for ways to make them memorize animal names and sounds faster. Instead, we let it build naturally and organically over time.

We teach these names and sounds in context. We see a cow and say, "That's a cow. It says moooo!" Eventually, the child makes the connection and picks it up. It's the same with

letters. When you see one say, "That's an M. It says mmmmm." One day, the connections will happen and they will memorize it.

No drill and kill in the early years. Just exposure.

Bottom line: stop worrying.

TAKEAWAY MESSAGE

Seriously, stop worrying. Consider this: when did you learn the ABCs or to count to 100? Remember, just like you're struggling to recall that information today or thinking of calling your parents to ask . . . that'll be your child in 30 years.

29

THE ONE WEIRD TRICK YOU'VE GOT TO TRY!

I love those online posts and headlines—you know, the clickbait ones. They are designed to make you want to click for more information soooo bad . . .

"She didn't know this one weird trick would change everything . . ."

"You won't believe what he saw next!"

"This will restore your faith in the world . . ."

Oh, they are so awful and yet, whoever came up with the concept is a genius. Humans are drawn to quick fixes, changes, and ways to make our lives better. We feel compelled to click and learn whatever promises to be life-changing (even when it's not and it's just seven pages of ads and a blurry photo).

Our drive to find hacks and fixes and workarounds in life trickles right on down the family ladder to our children.

Same spot, same kids. The play looks a little different than it used to . . . but also exactly the same.

We want to find the tricks for developing their skills.

We want to figure out how to raise kids to be the best and brightest.

We want the crazy tip that will help our kids succeed in academics, social skills, and all of life in general.

Well, guess what?

You won't believe this one weird trick to raising smarter, more confident, well-rounded kids.

Let them play.

Good old-fashioned play.

My motto: look past the mess and see the learning . . .
(Oh and they totally cleaned this up)

The miracle fix, the weird trick to learning, the life-changing step we can take with our kids is simply valuing play and honoring the child's need for it. That's it.

We live in a world that is moving so fast. Kids are being pulled this way and that, and we fill their days with clubs and sports and classes and all sorts of extras in a (sadly) misguided attempt to make them into better people. The problem is, children don't need all those extras to become great. They just need play.

When a child is playing, they are practicing high-level thinking skills and social skills. They're learning about cause and effect. They're developing problem-solving skills, critical thinking skills, and divergent thinking skills. It's almost surreal the amount of learning that comes from play.[10]

---

10 Singer DG, Golinkoff RM, Sharp HR. Play = Learning: How Play Motivates and Enhances Children's Cognitive and Social-Emotional Growth. Oxford University Press; 2006. https://books.google.com/books?id=9NFIuO7WrdwC&dq=effects+of+play+in+early+childhood&lr=&source=gbs_navlinks_s.

While we know in our hearts that children learn through play, there is an inherent problem for adults to overcome: we can't see the learning and we don't understand it.

Our society today values learning that is quantifiable. We need data. We test based on standards. We have benchmarks.

The learning that a child gets from play can't be measured and we are asked to instead blindly believe and assume the child is learning. This can feel problematic for today's parents.

In the culture of standardized testing, play doesn't seem like enough. If we can't see the learning and touch the learning and measure the learning, how can we be sure it's there? That doubt has led us to over-value tangible skills (such as learning letters and numbers) and undervalue important intangible skills that happen during play—personal skills, social skills, and life skills.[11]

An adult can set a preschooler down and rigorously teach them the letters of the alphabet through memorization tactics and direct instruction teaching. There's measurable data on progress made and the skill can be assessed. The test will end with hard facts: this is how many letters the child knows.

On the flip side, adults aren't in control during play and they can't chart play progress. The power here shifts to the child. This is often scary and difficult for parents and caregivers. At the end of play, there's no real assessment that can be taken and all data is casually observed without a formal assessment.

There is no standardized test for sharing.

You can't chart progress toward reasoning.

We have no data for empathy.

11 Nicolopoulou A. The alarming disappearance of play from early childhood education. Human Development. 2010;53:1–4. DOI: 10.1159/000268135. https://www.researchgate.net/publication/247701873_The_Alarming_ Disappearance_of_Play_from_Early_Childhood_Education/link/0046353be8511b27d0000000/download.

When a child is placed in all the clubs, sports, classes, and extras we can find—we have removed real chances for them to learn through uninterrupted, child-led play. Instead, they're left with only scripted experiences under the watchful eye and instruction of an adult.

As the push toward teaching academic skills to younger children has become more pervasive, their right to play has dwindled. There isn't enough time for play.[12] There's too much academic learning to be done. For the child who sits in preschool working on number flash cards— what play skills is that child sacrificing to sit there? What else could they be doing with their time that would be far more valuable for their future?

We've gotten it all backward.

This looks right.

Play teaches kids the immeasurable soft skills that will carry them through the hard academics and life trials of their future.[13] A child who has learned risk management on the playground knows exactly where their personal limits are. The teen who has built resilience from playing with trial and error as a child knows that failure isn't the end.

Our job as parents doesn't have to be this hard. We've put so much pressure on ourselves to make certain our kids are learning—but our kids already know exactly how to do this. They know it happens through play. We can go back to trusting our kids. We were trusted as children and our parents were trusted as children and their parents before them—we were trusted to learn through play. What a crazy weird trick to just go back to the way things had been.

12 Nicolopoulou A. The alarming disappearance of play from early childhood education. Human Development. 2010;53:1–4. DOI: 10.1159/000268135. https://www.researchgate.net/publication/247701873_The_Alarming_Disappearance_of_Play_from_Early_Childhood_Education/link/0046353be8511b27d0000000/download.

13 Rock L, Crow S. Not Just "Soft Skills": How Young Children's Learning & Health Benefit from Strong Social-Emotional Development. Too Small to Fail; 2017. http://toosmall.org/reso urces/TSTF-SED-Whitepaper.pdf.

Think of your child learning to walk. They didn't learn through flash cards. You didn't buy a computer program designed to teach them walking skills faster. You didn't read books about things you can do to help your child learn to walk more efficiently. What did you do? You trusted your child and you trusted the process and you watched in amazement as they developed this skill naturally.

If you're looking for that one weird trick to help your kids develop and grow into amazing people, shift your focus to play. Place a heavy value on play and reschedule your life to honor the time your child needs to do their most sacred work. Our kids need to be left to play without coaches or parents or teachers involved. Just play.

I don't remember ever being asked at a job interview how old I was when I learned to read or what year it was that I could count to 10. I was asked how I work on a team and what I would do if conflict arose. I was asked about my social, emotional, and life skills. It's funny how as adults, we rarely focus on academic skills, and instead look closely at people's personal skills.

With our own children and their education, it's harder to put that all into practice. We want so badly to have our hands in every pot, stirring things up just right for our kids. But the best we can do is refocus our values and go back to a time when kids were allowed to learn through play, without any reservations.

Let the children play.

LET'S GO BACK TO THE TWO Es

Remember how I told you about the two Es (see page 239)? So many of the exposures and experiences kids have through play in early childhood will help them grow in their academic learning. They learn about spatial awareness from puzzles. Math lessons are embedded into everything a child builds. Acting out social scenes builds their communication skills for future debates. Play serves as the best facilitator for the important exposures and experiences kids will draw on in the school years.

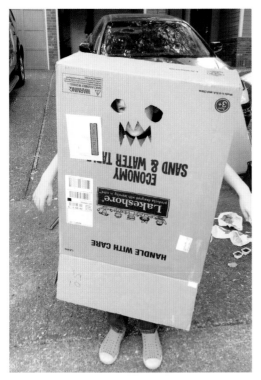

Kids and boxes. End of story.

Kate was here.

LET'S TALK PLAY (SOME MORE)

When I'm thinking about play, I break things down into these terms:

- **Free play.** Play where a child is free to make their own choices and decisions. This is very different from play at sports practice or dance classes where there are guidelines set by adults. Free play is the child having an open-ended experience.

- **Solo play.** Playing when a child is alone. This does not necessarily mean they are unsupervised.

- **Social play.** Play that happens with other children. Children might watch other children, play side by side, or interact.

HOW DO YOU HELP A CHILD PLAY?

Play is a skill children begin to develop at birth. Some kids seem born with a few more natural play skills than others while some need a bit of help learning to develop it. Remember, play can be learned—it's never too late to help a child find their play.

Real play happens independently of adults. As hard as that might be to comprehend, all play is not created equally and the most important play happens when children are without adults (that doesn't necessarily mean they aren't supervised, just that the parent is not an active player). We want the child to be actively in control of their play, not relying on adults to sit and facilitate. That's not easy for all kids and we can help them learn to do this.

Here are my tips for teaching kids how to play:

- **Make play a priority, not an afterthought.** Make time for play. Be conscious of how much playtime you provide each day. Kids can't learn a skill if they don't have time to develop it. Dedicate playtime time each day the same way you dedicate time for other activities.

- **Value play.** We need to make sure we value play and don't use it as a random afterthought or a way to dismiss the kids. "Just go play!" sends the wrong message. Show your children with all your words and tone of voice and body language that you value play.

- **We can exercise and grow the skill.** Start with small amounts of time and let your child know the expectation. "I am going to unload the dishwasher. Where will you be playing?" This lets the child have some understanding of how long they need to occupy themselves, where you will be, and what the reunification plan is. Gradually, this helps them build up stamina for longer self-entertainment.

- **Manage your play expectations.** Play is a skill that grows over time. We need to manage our expectations of what play will look like for our kids depending on both their age and their ability level. When a child is starting out in play (whether by age or because this is a new skill), start small. Aim for five minutes at a time. Increase the time expected as your child develops this skill.

- **Check your toys—they matter.** Not all toys are created equally and not all toys will help our kids find the kind of free play they so badly need. Avoid "one-and-done toys" that have batteries, flashing lights, and talk at our children. The shelf life of those toys is so short and they typically can be used only in one way, or they tell our children how to play. Shift the focus to simpler, open-ended toys that will grow with your child, like blocks, play kitchens, houses, cars and trucks, and toy animals. These toys breed play.

- **Cut out the unused toys.** The number of toys a child has doesn't matter—it's the quality of the toys that makes a difference. Finding the right toy to play with can be overwhelming if the shelves are full and the bins are overflowing. Pare down the collection until you have only the toys your child actually plays with. Make it an inviting space. Give them room to play and breathe. Donate old and unused toys often.

- **Help your child get started.** Figuring out how to start playing independently can sometimes be overwhelming for a child. That's where we can help! Help your child get started with their play by saying something like, "What happens if the dinosaurs decide to have picnic?" and let your child run with it (as you slowly back away and shift your focus elsewhere).

- **Remind kids that play is their job, not yours.** Be honest with your kids. "Play is your job and the best way for your brain to grow." Remember that play is not the work of adulthood, it's the job of children. We put so much pressure on ourselves to be in charge of play but this is their job. Remind them of that and then make yourself busy (you can't sit on the couch scrolling social media while telling the kids to work . . .). Plus (trust me here), no one wants to play with the parent cleaning a toilet.

- **Cut back on screen time.** Screen time significantly affects how well kids play. It truly does change their brains and makes it harder for them to play. If your child is struggling with play, audit their use of screen time and see if a change is needed (see page 276 for my tips on screen time).

Play is a skill—it's not just something kids do. It's valuable, important, and worth every amount of effort you put into it. It really is that important.

The big kids are playing together. Matt is playing with a bag. It's all play.

I call this photo: "A lesson in risk management." Sam felt safe so I felt safe.

TOYS MAKE PLAY

Toys are the tools for play in early childhood, but some toys are truly better tools than others. Avoid unnecessarily large toys that take away play space. Steer clear of battery-operated toys that sing songs or ask questions or do the work for the child. Instead, look for toys that have unlimited play potential, years of play life, and were probably something you or your parents had as a child.

The best toys fall into these categories:

- Building (blocks, marble runs, train sets)

- Acting out real-life scenes (play kitchens, doll houses and fire stations)

- Practicing empathy and care (dolls, figurines of animals or people)

- Imaginary and dramatic play (dress-up clothing, tools)

- Movement toys (cars, trucks, balls)

30

WHAT IS KINDERGARTEN READINESS?

HOW DO WE HELP KIDS BE READY FOR KINDERGARTEN?

We now arrive at the to *their first day of school* part. We've made it. We've gone from their first "no" to their first day of school. I'm like the dancing lady emoji right now.

Some of the best years of my life were spent teaching kindergarten. There is a buzz of electricity in kindergarten that can't be matched in other grades—the freshness of their minds, the wonder of "big kid school," and the wide-ranging ability levels. Kindergarten is special. Parents feel it, teachers feel it, kids feel it.

As we prepare to send our children off into the world of kindergarten—we often pause and wonder, "Are they ready for this? Are they ready for kindergarten? Will they be OK?!"

Teaching about fairy tales in 2008. There's nothing like kindergarten.

We want our kids to be successful.

We want our kids to be confident.

We want our kids to thrive in kindergarten—no one wants it to be an insurmountable struggle.

In an effort to help our kids have the best first year of school possible, the concept of "kindergarten readiness" became all the rage in the United States. The idea is that kids need to complete a checklist of skills before entering kindergarten (or rather *should* in order to be successful in class).

The problem is—and this goes along with the trends of today— the list of kindergarten readiness skills has become increasingly academic. And while kids are entering kindergarten knowing more academic skills than they did 30 years ago, they are lacking in so many other areas.

We can change this for our kids.

As you think about getting your child ready for kindergarten and what skills they'll need to be successful, I ask (as a former kindergarten teacher and from the bottom of my heart) that you consider so much more than just the academic development of your child.

The morning Sam left for kindergarten and asked for a "quick hold" on the couch…

Consider the whole child.

Consider day-to-day life in a classroom.

Consider what skills they'll need to learn all the amazing teachings in kindergarten.

> **Kindergarten is about so much more than just academic development. It's about a child leaving home and growing in their independence, taking a step out the door, and starting to have a little space away from their parents.**

This is a big step.

Academics won't prepare our children to face a day away from home. Knowing their letters won't make them more comfortable at school. Being able to count to 100 won't help them build relationships.

But there are skills that will help them as they start out on this independent life and navigate the world without us. It's scary for us. It's also scary for them, and we need to recognize all the social and life skills needed for this big moment. It's a big deal.

In these early years before kindergarten, during kindergarten, and even beyond, help your kids develop these skills to make those steps away from home just a little easier and a tad more tolerable. When you know your child has the truly important skills to succeed in school, you'll feel more confident letting go a little.

And they'll feel more confident walking through that new classroom's door.

THE REAL KINDERGARTEN READINESS SKILLS

Guess what? A lot of what I said throughout this book comes together here as part of school readiness. Because from day one with our children, we are working toward an end goal—which is to make sure they can live happy lives *away from us*, not just at home with us. Everything we do is part of a long parenting game to raise confident and independent people.

Here's my list of "non-academic and way more important skills" for kids entering kindergarten:

- **Ask for help from an adult who isn't a relative (communication skills)**

  Lots of adults are at school, and being able to ask for help, talk to them, and listen to them is a big deal. Problems arise at school, oftentimes outside of the classroom. It's critical your child is comfortable asking for help from a volunteer or recess teacher they might only vaguely know.

  Help your child learn to talk to adults. Model this behavior on outings by talking to cashiers and workers, and encouraging your kids to do the same (see Chapter 24 on taking kids in public).

- **Follow multi-step directions (listening skills)**

  Can your child follow multi-step directions? "Take off your coat, put it in the closet, and join me at the table." School is full of multi-step tasks and so is life. Being able to remember a set of instructions and finish a task fully is huge. Big time listening skills are also rooted in this, which are paramount to success. (Kids can practice these skills using any of the activities I've included in this book.)

- **Try two or three strategies to solve a peer conflict (problem-solving skills**

  It's easy for kids to walk up to a parent whenever there's an issue and have the parent swoop in with solutions and ideas, and magically fix it. But that's not how school or the real world work.

  Our kids need to have a toolbox of ideas for solving problems with peers before adult intervention. Have you taught your child to do this? Have you let them solve peer arguments? How do they handle disagreements with friends? (See Chapter 22 about how to teach kids conflict resolution skills—these help with peers too).

- **Ask questions when they need more information (questioning skills)**

  I used to tell my students that smart people got that way because they ask questions. They don't sit there. They don't hang their head when they don't get it. Smart people ASK. They seek information.

  Make sure your child asks questions, especially for clarification if they don't understand something. Model how to ask questions and think out loud when they're around. Show them how important it is to ask questions and get clarification. Watch how this skill builds through play as children test and retest theories, and question how things work.

- **Share and take turns with communal toys (social skills)**

  In Chapter 22, I talked about kids and sharing. School is built around communal materials and equipment, which is different than at home. There's always a bit of a gray area in sharing when objects have no clear owner.

Make sure your child understands how to handle communal property. Do they know how to wait for a turn? Do they know how to ask for a turn? Are they identifying when someone else is waiting? Teach your child how to share items in open spaces without taking all the time for themselves.

- **Win and lose graciously (empathy and social skills)**

This is a big one.

Kids have to learn how to both win and lose respectfully. Please let your child lose. Don't let them win at games every single time. They will not win at everything in school and that is a hard lesson to learn with 20 other kids staring back at them.

Not always winning is a lesson every child needs to learn. What happens if they don't learn this lesson? How is their self-esteem later in life when they do lose? Have they mistakenly made a connection between self-worth and winning?

Conversely, we need to teach children to win graciously and respectfully They need to understand that winning is part of the game, but the fun was in the playing.

- **Be self-motivated to learn (play skills)**

The goal is for kids to be self-motivated learners. We want them to thirst for knowledge, hunt down understanding, and drive their own education. They learn to do this through play, and then translate it to the classroom. Children who first learned through play are more intrinsically motivated to learn. They know how to problem solve, experiment on their own, dig deeper to find knowledge, and don't get discouraged when things are overly easy or overly complex. They see the learning possibilities in every task.

One big concern for parents is children being bored at school. Remember, a child who is bored at school is not necessarily an unchallenged child or a gifted child— being bored is not an indication of intellect. Part of what contributes to a child being bored at school is missing self-motivation skills. We want to raise children with drive and passion for learning, and we can do this by simply encouraging them to play in early childhood. (See Chapter 29 for more on play skills).

- **Be able to play within a set of rules (self-control skills)**

  Schools have rules. Classrooms have rules. Playgrounds have rules.

  Understanding that rules and boundaries exist to keep ourselves, others, and our surroundings safe is so important. School isn't a free-for-all, and all kids are beholden to the same expectations. It is critical our kids come into school knowing the basic rules of society, understanding why rules are in place, and knowing that boundaries are important.

  It is a shock to the system for a child entering school to have never experienced any sort of rule or consequence being enforced. Raising children who understand firm, clear, and consistent boundaries makes for a smoother transition into classroom life (and real life). (See Chapter 16 on how I use sensory bins to explicitly teach rules and boundaries).

- **Know how to fail and how to try again (resiliency skills)**

  This has far-reaching implications into adulthood and is so important. Let's have resilient kids. Let's raise kids who know that failing happens, it isn't the end of the world, and it means you get to try again. It's OK to fail.

  Help your child learn strategies to handle the disappointment.

  Help your child understand that failure isn't a reflection of who they are as a person.

  Help your child see the chance and beauty in hard work and trying. (See Chapter 13 where I talk about how saying yes more often and letting kids make decisions can help with their understanding of failure.)

Remember, the best way to introduce and hone all of these skills is through play.

You can't use flash cards to teach a child to handle losses.

There's no worksheet that explains sharing.

Internet videos are not going to empower your kids to be resilient.

As our children inch closer to their independent lives, think about the skills they truly need to be successful. Think long term. Think beyond tomorrow. Let's think about how to make them life ready, not just kindergarten ready.

SIMPLE READINESS SKILLS

Simple skills that are fantastic to have before entering kindergarten to promote independence and confidence:

- Put on a coat. Bonus: zip it up without adult help.
- Put on shoes correctly (tying shoes is tough, no worries there).
- Be fully toileted, which means knowing how to wipe.
- Know their first and last name. Bonus: know YOUR first and last name.
- Recognize their name in print.
- Write their first name (all capitals and backward letters is fine).
- Know how to use scissors.
- Know how to use a glue stick.

TAKEAWAY MESSAGE

Our job in early childhood isn't to get our kids ready for kindergarten, it's to get them ready for life beyond us. This is our real job—to prepare them for their future selves and their future lives, by giving them the tools to be incredible people who can stand tall and proud without us.

31

LEARNING ACTIVITIES

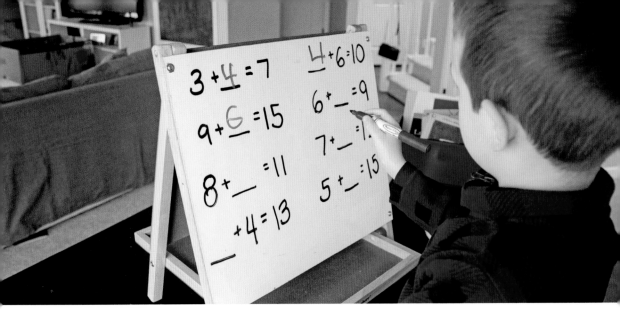

All activities are learning activities, so I've actually always hated this term.

How's that for an award-winning introduction?

This set of activities is full of serious fun and serious learning opportunities. Remember, when we sit a child down and force them to memorize a fact before they are ready—that's not best practice and it's not what the child needs.

Once a child has mastered a fact-based skill, we can use those facts to have some fun. Activities are a great way for a child to play with, practice, and continue growing their skills.

Activities are also awesome for giving kids exposure and experiences (remember the two Es from page 239?). We can use activities as a fun way to interact with concepts and skills, building their background knowledge and familiarity.

Hands-on activities are the best way to play with new information, especially for young children.

WARNING

All activities need to be done under direct adult supervision. Use discretion for what is safe for your child and home. Reach out to your pediatrician if you have any questions about your child's safety with an activity.

STICKER NAME SORTING

SUPPLIES

- Dot stickers
- Construction paper
- Painter's tape
- Marker

HOW-TO

On the construction paper, write out your child's name. Tape the paper to the wall. On some sheets of dot stickers, write all the letters of your child's name. Hand your child the sheet and let them sort out the letters of their name onto the paper.

WHY IT'S GOOD

It's fine motor skills, it's sorting, and it's letter recognition through your child's name. Your child's name will most likely be the first word they can read, so those letters are often the first letters your child will memorize. It all goes hand in hand.

WHAT ELSE

You can vary the complexity of this activity with how you write the letters on the stickers. You can write all the letters in order on the sticker sheet or mix them up. This simple twist changes the challenge level immensely.

SHAPE SORTING

SUPPLIES

- Painter's tape
- Various toys or other materials with clearly defined shapes

HOW-TO

On your floor, tape three shapes: circle, square, and triangle. Gather a large number of shape specific toys and objects. First, remind your child about some of the basic attributes for each shape (for example, a triangle has three sides and three points). Have your child sort the objects by which shape it goes with.

WHY IT'S GOOD

In this activity, we are asking a child to make real-world connections to shapes. Children use their visual discrimination skills to determine the shape of the object and classify the toy as such.

WHAT ELSE

Tape on the ground is a great way to define a learning space. Having a clear area for sorting makes this activity really doable.

COUNTING TO 100

SUPPLIES

- Tape
- Large piece of paper
- Stickers

HOW-TO

On your large piece of paper, make 10 boxes to count into. Inside each box, ask your child to put 10 stickers. Once they finish, work together to count all 100 stickers.

WHY IT'S GOOD

This activity helps children visualize the number 100 and makes counting up to it more manageable. Talk to your child about the patterns in the number words and about what 100 looks like. Having children see 100 helps them to visualize a very abstract concept as they ultimately learn that numerals have value.

WHAT ELSE

Does 100 always look the same? Find out by repeating this activity with other objects. Always start with the 10 boxes and count 10 items into each. Try coins, cereal, blocks, and other small toys.

SOUND MATCHING BIN

SUPPLIES

- Storage bin
- Uncooked rice
- Construction paper
- Toys and other items
- Black permanent marker

HOW-TO

Gather various toys and items from around the house. On construction paper, write down the first sound of each object (for example, b = ball, c = card). Place all the objects in the storage bin along with the uncooked rice. Have your child sort through the bin to find the objects and match them to the correct initial sound.

WHY IT'S GOOD

Hearing the first sound in a word is an unbelievably important pre-reading skill, as is isolating all sounds in a word. This is a big step on the road to reading.

WHAT ELSE

Play this activity again but focus on ending sounds and finally middle sounds. I can't stress enough how important it is for kids to hear sounds in words.

MATCHING EQUATIONS

SUPPLIES

- White butcher paper
- Sticky notes
- Black permanent marker

HOW-TO

On white butcher paper, write the numbers 1 through 10. On sticky notes, make equations to match the sums on the paper. Place the sticky notes on a table or hide them around a room for your child to find and match.

WHY IT'S GOOD

This is a movement and math activity. It gives kids a chance to work on their addition skills while engaging their whole body.

WHAT ELSE

Before kids are ready for this activity, they need to already have a solid conceptual understanding of addition and what it means to join numbers. Here they are working on the rapid recall of math facts.

ABC SORTING

SUPPLIES

- Alphabet magnets
- Colored bowls
- Tongs (optional)

HOW-TO

Pour all the alphabet magnets into one large bowl and ask your child to sort the magnets by color into the other bowls. Have them use plastic tongs to grab the letters and sort them into the correct colored bowl.

WHY IT'S GOOD

This activity asks children to sort letters by color—and distinguish one color from other colors. It also gives them an organic interaction with letters, which they may not recognize yet (my son did not know his letters in this photo). Using tongs turns this into a fine motor activity and helps develop a strong grip.

WHAT ELSE

Sorting is a powerful tool to use with kids, but remember, they don't need to just sort by color. Kids can sort by shape, texture, sound, and other attributes.

FIND THE SHAPE

SUPPLIES

- Painter's tape
- White butcher paper
- Crayons

HOW-TO

Roll out a large strip of white paper. On the paper, draw several shapes in various sizes and orientations. Ask your child to follow your verbal directions: "Color the circles purple." "Color the squares red." "Color the rhombus blue." (On behalf of all geometry teachers around the world, please help your child learn that a rhombus is a shape and a diamond is a stone). Repeat for all the shapes.

WHY IT'S GOOD

First, this activity asks a child to follow a two-part direction. They need to find the shape AND color it accordingly. They also need to transfer knowledge of shapes based on size ("is it still a triangle when it's tiny?"). Finally, this activity asks a child to work on a vertical surface, which promotes arm strength.

WHAT ELSE

It doesn't always have to be about finding shapes. You can set it up as Find the Names—using names in your family—and Find the Sight Words (or three-letter words when a child is growing in their reading skills).

BUILDING NAMES

SUPPLIES

- Painter's tape
- White butcher paper
- Small sticky notes (or sticky notes cut in half)

HOW-TO

Roll out a large strip of white paper. On the paper, write out your child's name several times— BUT with letters missing. Vary which letters are missing and how many are missing. On sticky notes, write down all the missing letters. Line the sticky note letters on the bottom of the paper or hide them around your house and ask your child to run and find the missing letters. When they find a letter, the child sticks it on a correct spot.

WHY IT'S GOOD

Understanding that letters work together to form words is a critical step in the reading process. Since the first word your child will learn to read is their name, this activity gives them a chance to see all the letters that work together to build their name.

WHAT ELSE

For school-aged children, this activity can be easily changed to Building Words (finding the missing vowel sound) or Building Sight Words.

ROLL AND TALLY

SUPPLIES

- Paper
- Marker
- Dice

HOW-TO

On the paper, draw a simple table for numbers one through six. Give your child a single dice and ask them to roll the dice, then put a tally mark in the corresponding column.

WHY IT'S GOOD

So. Much. Math. The child is learning about record keeping and data analysis, statistics, and probability. They're also working on numeration, the rapid recall of a group of objects without counting each one—it's how we adults instantly know six on a dice and don't need to count it each time.

WHAT ELSE

In this activity, do not ask your child to bundle their tallies in groups of fives. That's a complicated skill for when they are older and learn to skip count. Focus on having them keep track of their dice rolls—our longest running sheet took almost a week and we rolled the dice more than 250 times.

GIANT WORD SEARCH

SUPPLIES

- Large piece of paper
- Construction paper
- Painter's tape
- Markers

HOW-TO

On a piece of construction paper, make a list of 15 to 20 words your child can read or recognize. Plan out the word search first on that same paper. Choose the number of letters across (I used 9 across) and the number of letters down (I used 13 down). Add in the words you chose, overlapping letters and varying orientation. Fill in the gaps with random letters. Transfer your plan to a large piece of paper, hang it on the wall with painter's tape, and list the words to find. Let your child work to find them.

WHY IT'S GOOD

Word searches are great for promoting visual discrimination and concentration skills in kids. The giant size of this one makes it so much fun.

WHAT ELSE

This activity has become a holiday tradition. I make one for every major holiday with seasonally specific words for my oldest. He loves this personal, homemade activity.

EPILOGUE

There's a myth nowadays that we need to be perfect parents . . . that we need to find this white whale of idyllic child-rearing and all march on the same path. It's a popular belief today that there is only one right way to parent.

That's just not true.

Not only will that kind of mentality set you up for feelings of failure and guilt, it won't lead to anywhere good. It'll disrupt your best-laid plans. It'll mute all your feelings of success. It'll crush your confidence.

Friends, my best parenting advice is this: find the best parenting *for you*.

Find the parenting that feels right to you and run with it. Put on blinders, listen to your gut, and walk with your head held high because you are your child's parent. You know what is best for them.

You know what is best for you.

You know what is best for your family.

You know what is best for your child.

Stop comparing your family to someone else's family because, trust me, that won't help. You'll end up spinning your wheels and living an untrue parenting journey that doesn't really fit.

We didn't always have social media telling parents all the wrong things they're doing and what the right things should look like. That's a horrible new "bonus" to parenting in our generation. Our parents didn't face a world that second-guessed all their decisions or whether their child ate enough of the rainbow today.

I want nothing more for you than a peaceful, pride-filled journey in parenting. A journey you feel good about. A journey you are proud of.

In an era full of parenting guilt, let's turn our backs to the noise and loudly say, "I'm doing the best I can for my child and I feel great about it."

Parenting can be as amazing as you thought it would be when you signed up for this job—if you let it be. It is as rewarding and humbling as it was for every generation of parents before us, but sometimes it can be so loud out there. Stop second-guessing yourself, stop beating yourself up, stop thinking you are any less of a parent than those around you.

You are a good parent.

You are the right parent for your child.

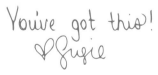

GLOSSARY OF SKILLS AND TERMS

Empathy: A child's understanding of another person's feelings, and their ability to read facial expressions, body language, and action.

Fine motor skills: Small, intricate movements of the hands. Skills like pinching, grasping, and finger work. Fine motor skill work helps promote handwriting and dexterity.

Gross motor skills: Large movements of the whole body. Skills like jumping, hopping, and running.

High-level thinking: Challenging thinking skills where the child is asked to explain, reason, create, or solve a problem.

Intrinsic motivation: A child's internal drive to learn a skill or master a task; their ability to continue to try to solve a problem or meet a goal.

Low-level thinking: Basic memorization, list-making, and recall skills.

Number recognition: Rapid recall of number names from sight.

Resilience: A child's understanding that failure is inevitable and doesn't define them; how willing they are to withstand a difficult task.

Rote: Fancy word for memorizing.

Sensory bin: Tactile learning station where a child interacts with a material to explore and discover using multiple senses.

Self-control: How well a child manages their impulses.

Spatial awareness: Understanding the location of an object in relationship to another; being able to rotate and translate a shape or object and understand it is still the same.

Visual discrimination: A child's ability to see the differences in objects and symbols that are closely related, like the letters p, b, d, or various shapes.

QUICK TIPS, TRICKS, AND SUSIE-SAYINGS

TRY AGAIN FOR GREATER SUCCESS

Have a kiddo who is testing the boundaries? Offer them a second chance to "try again for greater success." If they can't handle it, invite them to walk away and try again another time. Consistent language ("let's try again for greater success") lets the child know this is their last opportunity before they miss out. I know "greater success" might seem like a big statement for a two-year-old, but kids understand big statements and big words. They'll come to learn exactly what you mean by that phrase.

WILLY WONKA PARENTING

Sometimes parenting doesn't go so hot. Sometimes, I know they should be acting a certain way (they do too), but they're not listening and I'm low on willpower—like when my kids decided to play "snakes" and slither on the mall floor. I knew they *should* stop, but I just didn't have the strength to handle it. I call this Willy Wonka parenting, as in "no . . . stop . . . don't." It's good for a parenting laugh.

Counting to 10 while laying on the floor of a playland. "No...stop...don't..."

THE OFFERING

Each night, right before bedtime, I sneak back into my kids' rooms and leave a little bowl of dry cereal and a sippy cup of water. I call this "the offering." It's my offering to them in exchange for a little peace in the morning and a touch of quiet. This gives them the bit of food they need to wake up happy and stay in their rooms to play. (Note: I only introduce this offering once my kids are old enough to eat unsupervised, and I only use cereal that does not pose a choking hazard.)

LUNCH AT BREAKFAST

One of the hardest parts of coming home from an outing is arriving at lunchtime with hangry kids. To help myself out, I started preparing *lunch* while the kids ate *breakfast*.

There's a lull and a calm while the kids eat at the table, so I pause for a half-second and make sandwiches then. I cut up fruit. I put it in a storage container in the fridge. When we come home at noon and it's bedlam, I can have lunch on the table in no time, without incident, and while still with my wits about me.

PARTY TRICK SKILLS

Party trick skills look great on paper or at a party, but they don't have any merit for a child's future success. They are typically memorizing skills like the ABCs, 123s, knowing the 50 states, or being able to name every planet in the solar system. They're good for a party trick, but they aren't a real indication of a child's intellect. Wouldn't it be amazing if we valued social and emotional skills the way we revere party trick skills? I'd love for someone to corner me at the punch bowl to watch their kid self-regulate . . .

THE MAGIC CARPET

The magic carpet is my front doormat. I introduced that term to my children in their toddlerhood as a central meeting location in our house before we leave. It can be exhausting wrangling up the kids to head out. Instead, I announce, "Meet me on the magic carpet" and they all head to a seated position in front of the door. This gives me a moment to assess the house and our supplies before we leave, and then we are on our way.

The magic carpet in action (not pictured, me running frantically around tidying up).

UNION BREAK

Also known as nap time. I treat nap time as my "union break" and I DO NOT do housework during that time. Just as workers outside the home have breaks and lunches and restroom stops during their day—this is my time (all at once). I firmly believe that children need to see parents cleaning up and tidying and be a part of that process. So if the house is always magically cleaned up during nap time, we lose a chance to teach those skills and instill in our children a sense of community and responsibility for the home. Instead, sit down and take your union break.

SCREENS AS A TOOL

My family is NOT a screen-free family. We are a screens-as-a-tool family.

This means, as parents, my husband and I choose when to turn screens on. We use them as a tool for when WE need help. We make the decision to turn on the TV or hand over a device—our children do not. It is OUR tool to use, not their tool to escape the hard work of play in childhood.

A few tips:

- Make screen time predictable. My kids know the TV will be on every morning while I make breakfast and will go off after breakfast is over. In a perfect day, that's the only time the TV is on unless something comes up and I make the choice to use my tool once again to help (for example, during dinner prep). Having a predictable screen time means my kids aren't worried about when they'll watch a show again. They know exactly when that will happen.

- Remember that all shows are not created equal and you are the gatekeeper to the shows your child watches. If you don't like a show, don't let them watch it.

- If screens have become a problem and are on too much for your family, make a change. You are the parent. My recommendation is to go cold turkey and turn the screens completely off for a few days. This will be hard on the first day but will get easier. When you decide to turn on the screens again, reintroduce them as your tool. Give clear and consistent boundaries. "We will watch one show. When this show is over, I will turn off the TV." Reclaim the screen as your tool.

- Remember, screens can be used as a parenting tool, but it should not be used for a child who wants to take the easy route and avoid playing. Play is serious work for kids and it's mentally taxing . . . that's actually a good thing. Emphasize the importance of play. Deemphasize the role of screens.

THE CLEANUP NUMBER

Telling a child to "clean up" might as well be said in a foreign language. The concept of cleaning up is too abstract and large, and if they can't determine an approach or place to start, they often give up. They have no idea how to just clean up. To help my kids have an understanding of how to clean up, I use a number system. This gives them purpose and a concrete goal. I survey the room and the damage and tell them a random number. "You need to clean up 12 things in this room." That's so much easier for them to understand. Suddenly, this large idea of "clean up" has become a more manageable 12 items.

For kids who are not counting yet, give a specific, single task. "Your job is to put the blocks in the basket." One single job is much easier to bite off than a playroom that needs to be completely cleaned up. "When you finish the blocks, I'll give you your next job."

PAPER CHAIN COUNTDOWN

Have an important event coming up? Vacation? Holiday? Visitor? Birthday? Make a paper chain countdown starting 15 to 20 days in advance. Let your child pull off one chain link every morning.

Time is an abstract concept for children. They can't relate to it or quantify it. By putting time in a concrete, "touchable" format like a paper chain, suddenly they can see the amount of time passing. This is huge. They have more independence and less anxiety about when the important event is going to happen.

The birthday countdown!

IN THIS FAMILY . . .

Our family is different from our neighbors, friends, and classmates. Rather than shifting the focus and saying "well, that's how they do things," I explain our policies and rules by saying that in this family . . . we have different rules from others and different expectations. I want to remind my children that we are a unit and a team, and it's OK for our life to look different than other families. When they complain or grumble about how so-and-so is allowed to do something, I say, "That's great for that family! In this family . . ." and we move on from there.

In this family, we make decisions that are best for us.

GET TO KNOW YOUR NEIGHBORS

Get outside. Knock on some doors. Get to know your neighbors. The single best parenting decision I ever made was consciously choosing to meet my neighbors. I lived on my street for five years before we had our first child. Until then, we knew one neighbor, and that was it. Our street was a dud. . . or so we assumed.

One day, we were coming back from infant swim class and realized one of the families from our class was following us. Nope. They lived four doors down and we had no idea we had babies born two months apart. We'd never met.

Later, when I had a 21-month-old and a 1-month-old, a family moved in across the street with two kids ages four and six. Close enough. I threw jackets on my kids and ran—I mean ran—to meet them. That was a life-changing day for me.

From then on, we all started playing in our FRONT yards, instead of the back. We got to know each other. We shared picnics in the yard. We took turns flipping burgers and suddenly, my dud-of-a-street turned out to be full of other families too. These families became our best friends and the "friend cousins" you dream of for your children. The kids range in age from 1 to 11 years old, but that doesn't matter.

Our paths never would have crossed except that we chose the same street to live on. We don't parent the same way, we don't have the same backgrounds, we don't lead the same lives. But we live on the same street.

We are neighbors. We help out. We are second families. What a gift we have given our children by going out on a limb to meet strangers. What a gift we have given ourselves.

Set your chair in the front yard. Say hi. Get to know your neighbors.

PAJAMAS TO GO

There's nothing worse than coming home from a fun evening event, the kids falling asleep in the car, and then having to wrangle them into pajamas while they're fussy and half asleep. Instead, bring pajamas to go.

Before you load the kids in the car, change them into their pajamas. Doing this one little step while the kids are awake and of sound mind and body . . . well, your future self will thank you. It's also a great move for kids who are used to a bedtime routine—you can do some of that routine before getting in the car.

PLAY, READING, AND CONVERSATION

Want a quick checklist of what kids need each day? Here it is: play, reading, and conversation. No matter how young or old your child is, this is what they need to grow, develop, and learn.

- Make sure your child is playing all day every day.

- Read books to them and surround them with good books to look through.

- Talk to them even if they can't talk back. Narrate your day.

Play, reading, and conversation—the secret to raising successful children is contained in a three-bullet checklist. Pretty cool, huh?

THE SUPPLY LIST

I don't keep a room full of supplies in my house. I don't have one of those fancy craft closets. I don't have a playroom or basement. What I do have is a small back corner of my laundry room where I store my meager supplies (for arts, crafts, and activities).

Here are my go-to, most used and loved supplies:

- Storage bins: small (17 quart), medium (28 quart) and large (41 quart—I call this my two buns bin)

- Uncooked rice (5 pounds)—sealed in a bag or container

- Dot stickers (0.75 inch)

- Construction paper

- Markers

- Crayons

- Large black marker

- Dot markers

- Washable paint

- Roll of white butcher paper

- Sensory bin supplies such as funnels, cups, jars, and scoops

- Sticky notes

- Painter's tape or other wall-safe tape

- Pom-pom balls (for children who are old enough; use good supervision)

Let's be real. Here's how my supplies actually look.

INDEX

pouring station: 135

preschool: 121, 233, 236, 245, 284

preschooler: 60, 77, 104, 106, 127, 201, 213, 244

problem-solving: 44, 71, 72, 139, 176, 177, 237, 243, 255

proof of mom: 217, 218, 220, 221, 222

pudding: 133

puzzle: 110, 112, 134, 246

ramp: 189

readiness: 252, 254, 258

reading: 40, 232, 234, 235, 236, 264, 267, 268, 279

recognition: 106, 261, 273

recycled: 44, 45, 52, 134, 156, 190

recycling: 190

rescue: 43, 139

responsibility: 19, 276

restaurant: 12, 56, 225, 228, 230

rice: 48, 109, 112, 118, 119, 120, 121, 122, 124, 126, 128, 129, 130, 133, 134, 138, 145, 148, 264, 280

routine: 15, 77, 167, 183, 201, 205, 215, 216, 279

rules: 19, 20

saying yes: 93, 95, 96

science: 107, 111, 119, 187, 189, 192

scientific: 51, 115

scissors: 2, 190, 258

scoop: 48, 109, 118, 134, 138, 141, 157, 281

scooping: 109, 119, 137, 138

screens-as-a-tool: 276

self-control: 55, 77, 88, 121, 122, 123, 127, 175, 184, 204, 237, 257

self-esteem: 94, 95, 237, 238, 256

self-motivated: 256

self-motivation: 238, 256

self-regulate: 275

self-regulating: 174, 237, 238

self-regulation: 88, 92

self-sufficient: 151

self-worth: 256

sensory: 48, 49, 105, 107, 111, 112, 117, 118, 119, 120, 121, 122, 123, 124, 125, 126, 127, 128, 129, 130, 131, 132, 133, 134, 136, 140, 141, 142, 148, 150, 155, 157, 187, 257, 281

shape: 106, 159, 160, 189, 195, 226, 229, 233, 262, 266, 267, 273

shapes: 77, 106

share: 8, 26, 60, 86, 115, 165, 167, 177, 178, 181, 182, 206, 225, 255, 256, 284

sharing: 19, 168, 181, 182, 255, 257

shopping: 55, 56, 63, 80, 89, 199, 201, 204

shredded paper: 136

sibling: 120, 162, 163, 168, 169, 170, 171, 172, 174, 178, 179, 180, 183, 187, 195, 224

sight words: 267, 268

sittervising: 150, 151, 152, 155, 158

snack: 15, 49, 98, 163, 208, 213, 215, 227

social-emotional: 236, 237, 243, 245

social: 8, 20, 121, 123, 146, 170, 182, 183, 199, 201, 232, 236, 237, 243, 244, 246, 247, 249, 254, 255, 256, 272, 275

socializing: 204

society: 199, 233, 244, 257

sorting: 108, 112, 116, 261, 262

sportsmanship: 230

stickers: 37, 51, 59, 108, 116, 195, 225, 226, 229, 261, 263, 280

sticky wall: 45

supply list: 280

survival mode: 143, 147

Susie-sayings: 274

tabies: 36, 37, 39, 40, 42, 44, 45, 46, 47, 48, 49, 50, 51, 52, 129, 130

taby: 5, 31, 34, 35, 36, 37, 38, 39, 40, 42, 43, 44, 45, 46, 47, 49, 50, 51, 52, 59, 60, 120, 125, 129, 130, 145

ABOUT THE AUTHOR

SUSIE ALLISON is an actual mom with three actual kids. She lives a happy life outside of Seattle where she and her husband raise their little family. Susie has a degree in elementary education and had a blast working as a kindergarten and first grade teacher (her dream job). After having a baby, leaving the classroom, and having another baby, Susie needed help making it to nap time each day. She realized she possessed a secret superpower to prevent time from ticking backward—making kid activities from household supplies.

Susie started Busy Toddler on Instagram in 2015 to share her easy activities with others, and by 2020, her account had over one million followers. Her advice inspires hundreds of thousands of parents, and her activities help countless children make it to their nap times. Susie also wrote the extremely popular homeschool preschool curriculum, Playing Preschool.

You can see more of Susie's activities and parenting tips on Instagram (@busytoddler) or on her website (BusyToddler.com).